Prais

*"If you want to know ......
Peggy will show you. Read this book and find out
about the one thing you need to know now!"*

— **Mark Victor Hansen**, the co-creator of the #1 *New York
Times* best-selling series *Chicken Soup for the Soul®*; co-author
of *Cracking the Millionaire Code, The One Minute Millionaire,*
and *Cash in a Flash;* and author of *Richest Kids in America*

---

*"The Won Thing is a book that many have been waiting for. It
offers one simple yet profound solution to living a life of greater
success and fulfillment. Read it and watch your life flourish!"*

— **Marci Shimoff**, the *New York Times* best-selling
author of *Happy for No Reason* and co-author
of *Chicken Soup for the Woman's Soul*

---

*"Simplicity at its best, **The Won Thing** could be
the <u>one</u> solution you've been waiting for to catapult
you from ordinary to extraordinary!"*

— **Bob Proctor**, the best-selling author of *You Were Born Rich*

---

*"Everyone's life is a journey of learning. Peggy McColl
opens her heart and shares her own remarkable story
and the events that led her to discover the one thing
(the secret to a fulfilling and successful life)."*

— **Bill Bartmann**, billionaire business coach

---

*"Peggy has distilled years of research and her own
practical application of these ideas into a book that's
easy to read and understand, and, most important, contains
guidance that anyone can use. This book is full of evidence
that anyone can learn and apply immediately to turbocharge
his or her life and propel it into the next level of success."*

— **John Assaraf**, the best-selling author of
Having It All: Achieving Your Life's Goals and Dreams

"**The Won Thing** answers the question many people have yearned to have answered . . . what is the 'one thing' that will make my life super successful? Peggy McColl is a master at cutting through the hype to reveal the truth! This book is a must-read!"

— **Crystal Andrus**, the best-selling author of
Simply . . . Woman! and *Transcendent Beauty*

"Peggy's genuine caring and knowledge are expressed on every page of this wonderful book, **The Won Thing**. Her enlightening approach will not only inspire you, it will surely help you discover the one thing."

— **Sandra Anne Taylor**,
the *New York Times* best-selling author
of *Quantum Success* and *Secrets of Attraction*

"Peggy McColl has created a brilliant, thought-provoking way to discover the secret of living an enriched life. Open this book immediately and put it to work in your life."

— **Gay Hendricks, Ph.D.**, the author of *The Big Leap: Conquer Your Hidden Fear and Take Life to the Next Level*

"If you want your life to finally make sense—if you want to know what that one thing really is, look no further than the pages within this book. **The Won Thing** may be the <u>one</u> solution you've been waiting for."

— **Arielle Ford**, the best-selling author of *The Soulmate Secret: Manifest the Love of Your Life with the Law of Attraction*

"For those of us who loved **Your Destiny Switch**, Peggy McColl has created (yet another) masterpiece. You are surely going to love **The Won Thing!**"

— **David Riklan**, the founder of **SelfGrowth.com**, the #1 self-improvement Website on the Internet

THE
WON
THING

ALSO BY PEGGY MCCOLL

BE A DOG WITH A BONE: Always Go for Your Dreams

21 DISTINCTIONS OF WEALTH:
Attract the Abundance You Deserve

YOUR DESTINY SWITCH: Master Your
Key Emotions, and Attract the Life of Your Dreams!

HAY HOUSE TITLES OF RELATED INTEREST

YOU CAN HEAL YOUR LIFE, the movie,
starring Louise L. Hay & Friends
(available as a 1-DVD program and an expanded 2-DVD set)
Watch the trailer at: **www.LouiseHayMovie.com**

THE SHIFT, the movie,
starring Dr. Wayne W. Dyer
(available as a 1-DVD program and an expanded 2-DVD set)
Watch the trailer at: **www.DyerMovie.com**

EXCUSES BEGONE! How to Change Lifelong,
Self-Defeating Thinking Habits, by Dr. Wayne W. Dyer

FROM STRESS TO SUCCESS . . . in Just 31 Days!
by Dr. John F. Demartini

HAPPINESS NOW! Timeless Wisdom for Feeling
Good FAST, by Robert Holden, Ph.D.

28 DAYS TO A MORE MAGNETIC LIFE,
by Sandra Anne Taylor

All of the above are available at your
local bookstore, or may be ordered by visiting:

Hay House USA: **www.hayhouse.com**®
Hay House Australia: **www.hayhouse.com.au**
Hay House UK: **www.hayhouse.co.uk**
Hay House South Africa: **www.hayhouse.co.za**
Hay House India: **www.hayhouse.co.in**

THE WON THING

*The "One" Secret to a
Totally Fulfilling Life*

PEGGY McCOLL

HAY HOUSE, INC.
Carlsbad, California • New York City
London • Sydney • Johannesburg
Vancouver • Hong Kong • New Delhi

Published and distributed in the United States by: Hay House, Inc.:
www.hayhouse.com • *Published and distributed in Australia by:* Hay
House Australia Pty. Ltd.: www.hayhouse.com.au • *Published and distributed in the United Kingdom by:* Hay House UK, Ltd.: www.hay
house.co.uk • *Published and distributed in the Republic of South Africa by:* Hay House SA (Pty), Ltd.: www.hayhouse.co.za • *Distributed
in Canada by:* Raincoast: www.raincoast.com • *Published in India by:*
Hay House Publishers India: www.hayhouse.co.in

Design: Tricia Breidenthal

Library of Congress Cataloging-in-Publication Data

McColl, Peggy.
  The won thing : the "one" secret to a totally fulfilling life / Peggy
McColl. -- 1st ed.
    p. cm.
  ISBN 978-1-4019-2466-9 (tradepaper : alk. paper) 1. Self-actualiza-
tion. 2. Goal (Psychology) 3. Success. I. Title.
  BF637.S4M2347 2009
  158--dc22
                                          2009009481

ISBN: 978-1-4019-2466-9

12 11 10 09   4 3 2 1
1st edition, September 2009

Printed in the United States of America

*To the one who
means everything to me:
my son, Michel.*

CONTENTS

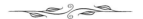

FOREWORD

As I read the manuscript for *The Won Thing* to get a feel for the essence of this book, I really felt more connected to Peggy than ever before. I've actually known her for a few years through our personal friends, as well as from both of us being a part of a small group of authors who "mastermind" weekly on how to help each other spread our messages of hope and success throughout the world.

What I discovered in reading *The Won Thing* is that almost every successful person learns his or her secrets by taking small, simple steps on a regular basis and not as a result of some *big* thing that suddenly happens.

Many of these principles have been passed down from generation to generation, but most people never apply what they learn—they just accumulate the information and never take action. My belief is that it's action that causes attraction, and it's doing things in the right order that makes all the difference in the world.

Peggy has faced the same problems as everyone else, yet she's decided to overcome those challenges and become the type of person who grows, learns, and takes action regardless of the circumstances.

This seems to be the common thread among highly successful people: they have a "no matter what" attitude, and Peggy certainly has that. I sensed throughout this book that anyone can follow its wisdom and succeed.

Although the title of this awesome book promises the "Won" thing, its real pearls are in the simplicity of its advice on learning how to think and act differently. If it's true that success leaves clues, then this book is full of evidence that anyone can learn and apply immediately to turbocharge his or her life and propel it into the next level of success. Peggy has distilled years of research and her own practical application of these ideas into a book that's easy to read and understand, and, most important, contains guidance that anyone can use.

I've been asked by thousands of people around the world what it takes to achieve success and can honestly say that the answer is quite simple: think and do a few critical things daily that will ensure success, and stop sabotaging yourself through thoughts and actions that cause chaos and destruction in your life.

Every chapter in this book will open your heart to a world of possibilities and give you a path to follow so that you, too, can reach the level of success you know is possible for you.

I had a sense from Peggy that she really has applied what she is writing about, and that her life has become a masterpiece by design . . . "Won" little piece at a time. Like a beautiful jigsaw puzzle, *The Won Thing* gives you all the pieces and instructions on how to create your own masterpiece.

I highly recommend that you read this book, apply what you learn, and share it with those you love.

— **John Assaraf**
New York Times best-selling author featured in
The Secret; founder, OneCoach

INTRODUCTION

I was sitting on my kitchen floor with my back against the dishwasher, staring forward at nothing as the tears rolled down my face. What was I going to do? I was a single mom trying to achieve success as an entrepreneur, and my life was a mess: I had overstretched my budget, had no income for months, feared I wouldn't be able to pay my bills given that I was almost out of money and credit, and didn't know how I was going to make my mortgage payment. I felt like it couldn't get any worse than this. How was I ever going to find the strength to get up off that floor? I was exhausted by stress and worn out by the demands of my life. If only there was one simple answer, one key that would end all my problems and lead me out of this prison of sadness and fear and into joy, fulfillment, and prosperity again.

Of course, I did find the strength to get up and move forward . . . and that's why I've written this book. What I learned along the way is something so powerful that I needed to share it with others. I discovered the one thing—or, as I call it, the "Won Thing"—that would allow me to win at life and create all that I want for myself.

I used to believe that life was like the board game we used to play as kids called, conveniently enough, *The Game of Life.* We'd move our little plastic cars that served as the playing pieces around the board, accumulating money, points, and children (little pink and baby blue pegs that we squeezed into the cars). It was a clever game that was designed to teach a formula for living the good life, requiring us to make decisions along the way. After playing it a few times, I figured out some winning strategies—by the time I reached that final square at the end of the winding trail, if I was smart and lucky, I could count up my pile of assets and feel like a success. I became determined, however, to know the secret to winning at the game of *real life:* the Won Thing.

The Big Questions

At some point every human being wonders, *How can I get my life to work for me? How can I end my discomfort and suffering?* Asking these questions is the first step on a spiritual journey of self-discovery in which we learn about ourselves and our relationship to everyone else who's on his or her own journey. The more we inquire, the more we begin to realize that life isn't about avoiding pain, but about knowing what we want for ourselves and then making it happen.

If we were chimpanzees, goldfish, spaniels, or cockatoos, we wouldn't ask ourselves the big questions about happiness, purpose, and meaning; nor would we create emotional suffering for ourselves or ponder how to make our lives better. We'd simply go through our days eating and sleeping, with no sense that our lives might serve some larger purpose. Life would consist of us doing our own "thing"—just like all the other animals around us—without a personal plan for happiness and success.

But being human means seeking relief from hardship and searching for answers as to how we can feel joyous, fulfilled, and at peace with our lives exactly as they are. We want to be as excited as a dog playing with a ball. Unlike animals, we pine for what we've lost and ache for what we don't have because we think about the past and the future far more than they do. Our minds create thoughts about our experiences, and these thoughts generate strong emotions that reinforce our beliefs.

Naturally, it's painful to lose something or someone we care about. But when we think that we'll never regain what we've had, and concentrate on how awful it is to be without a person or situation in the present, we create suffering for ourselves. We jump to what should be and what ought to have been, and shift away from the present moment. While that dog plays, totally focused on what it's doing, our minds are wandering off in every direction, formulating thoughts that produce painful feelings.

Even when we're not feeling the pain of loss or lack, our minds are busy developing restless opinions. We don't want to spend each day doing the same thing. We're programmed to be curious, to strive for fulfillment. We long for lives that are more interesting and meaningful. We want to feel that we matter, that the world wouldn't be the same place if we weren't in it. We want to contribute in a lasting way, whether it's by creating something that continues on after we're gone or loving people so deeply that they remember us with a big smile years after we've passed.

As we ask questions and seek our purpose, we look for answers both inside and outside of ourselves. We learn from others; our own experiences; books, workshops, teachers, and mentors; and our painful mistakes. We receive many messages—some of them mixed—about

what we're supposed to be doing with our lives and what will make us feel as if we're on the right path toward happiness, fulfillment, and a sense of meaning.

In this age of information, we're continually bombarded with ideas and choices. All the guidance, advice, opportunities, and possibilities can be overwhelming. There are multitudes of alternatives available to us. Just choosing which cereal to buy at the supermarket can be overwhelming. We scan the shelves and see a virtual wall of various brands, shapes, and sizes—how on earth are we supposed to figure out what to do with our lives when we can't decide something as meaningless as this? Many of us long to simplify matters and find the "one thing" that will ease our discomfort, create a sense of bliss and clarity, and make us feel that our lives have meaning and that we're living authentically and according to our strongest values.

My Search for the Won Thing

As a young woman, I longed to find the path to personal success, to the Won Thing: that one, secret key that would release me from the prison of my emotional pain and lead me to a better, more fulfilling life. I began a three-decade-long journey of discovery and introspection that took me from weekend seminars to weeklong retreats. I devoured inspirational audio recordings and self-help books, wrote and recited affirmations, formulated my mission statement, and vowed each day to improve myself and try harder to make my life work.

I truly believed that my determination to stay on the path of self-development had placed me in the fast lane to success. Even so, I had an urge to progress even faster and leave my problems in the dust, growing smaller in my rearview mirror as I sped forward. I decided that my vehicle, my *self,* was the only thing holding me back. I needed to soup it up! If I could transform myself into a Lamborghini of success, I'd fly down the highway toward perfection.

What I lacked, or so it seemed, was the one thing that would dramatically change myself, and therefore, my life. I was certain that this key existed, and if I spent enough time searching for it, I'd find it. Discovering this simple answer would allow me to say good-bye to a life of uncertainty, confusion, unhappiness, and low self-esteem for good—no longer weighed down by troubles. Aerodynamically flawless, I'd zip down that highway and reach my resting spot, my personal heaven, in no time. My destination was a point in my life, somewhere out there in the distance, where I could be permanently happy, content, and free from all struggles and sadness.

This book is the story of my search. Within these pages, I share the wisdom I've absorbed from many great motivational speakers and teachers. I explain what I know about some of the most highly touted cures for unhappiness and lack of personal success, and why each of these magic potions had something wonderful to offer me but didn't turn out to be the one thing that took me where I wanted to go.

After a very long search, I *did* find the one thing . . . and I'll tell you what that is. But first, to truly appreciate it and know how to use it properly, you must go on a journey. I won't require you to commit 30 years, count-less weekends, or thousands of dollars, as I did. I'll only ask that you follow the story of my own experience, read

about the lessons I learned, and start thinking about how you can apply them in your own life. I know that by walking this path with me for a short time, you'll better understand what I call the "Won Thing" when it's revealed to you.

So bring your curiosity, and your willingness to make some changes in your life, and come along with me. I hope to be a good traveling partner who can amuse you with my stories, and I promise that in the end you'll understand why I've taken you on back roads and side trips on the way to your destination: the Won Thing.

PART I

MOVING FROM THE "ONE THING" TO THE "WON THING"

Chapter One

RESCUE ME!

"No one is going to come and rescue you."

— FROM *WHAT COLOR IS YOUR PARACHUTE?*
BY RICHARD NELSON BOLLES

Like many people, I used to dream of having someone swoop in and fix all of my problems for me. I was young and it was the 1970s, when the women's movement was just starting to awaken people to the idea that women didn't necessarily need a man to be happy. Personally, I didn't agree with the popular T-shirt that said: A WOMAN WITHOUT A MAN IS LIKE A FISH WITHOUT A BICYCLE. After all, when I was in love with my first boyfriend in high school, I walked around in a state of sheer happiness. My life seemed complete . . . until that day when

he broke up with me and I fell into the depths of despair. Being just a teenager, I felt this was the end of the world. The way I saw it, he'd loved me, and that meant I was lovable; so when he left me, well, that must have meant that somehow I'd become *un*lovable.

Of course, as I got older, I realized that there would be other boyfriends. My subsequent relationships taught me that after the dizzy feeling of being infatuated fades away, every partnership proves to have its own set of challenges. I discovered that I was still capable of loving and being loved, yet a romantic partner wasn't the answer to all my problems after all.

For a while, I believed that my career was the answer: if I were making lots of money and achieving success, certainly I'd be rescued from unhappiness. Starting as a teenager, I worked hard in various jobs, from secretary to computer demonstrator to salesperson. I had my own apartment and a nice car and was doing really well, especially considering that I hadn't started out with money, a family name, or an impressive degree (in fact, I never went to college). I figured that I'd assembled all the pieces of a fulfilling and wonderful life . . . so why was I feeling so unsettled? That desire for someone, or something, to free me from all my emotional pain didn't go away.

In those days, I was insecure in my relationships. I was making good money but was often dissatisfied with my jobs, thinking, *When is my life going to come together in the way it's supposed to?* I truly believed that out there somewhere was the one thing that would end all my suffering and help me conquer the game of life. I needed to know the secret strategy for personal success.

Whether it's a romantic partner, a successful career, or the windfall from a lottery, the ultimate antidote to

unhappiness is what most people long for. Especially when we're in crisis, the idea of a quick fix or that recipe for instant relief can be very attractive. Often, when we have a very bad cold or flu, we're tempted to reach for that bottle on the drugstore shelf that promises to relieve every possible symptom, including ones we don't have! We just want the discomfort and misery to go away.

Pain and suffering can be great motivators for seeking relief—no wonder we look to love, careers, or money as the perfect tonic. We're just searching for the one thing that will cure our loneliness, insecurity, unhappiness, fear, and uncertainty.

Prince Charming to the Rescue

Human beings are social creatures, so we try to connect with others and deepen our relationships when we're feeling lonely. But that *feeling* of loneliness is one that we can experience even when we're around other people. It's an emotion created in ourselves in response to thought patterns that are unhealthy and distorted. When we're insecure, believing that we're inadequate and even unlovable, someone may say, "You are wonderful and beautiful," and we might think, *How can he be so blind? Of course I'm not!* No amount of praise from anyone will rescue us from unworthiness unless we choose to change our mind-sets and emotions. Our own ability to sabotage and keep ourselves feeling bad is no joke. There are even fashion models who appear on magazine covers who *still* think they aren't beautiful!

The yearning to escape painful feelings leads us into rebound relationships, partnerships, or marriages that

are all wrong. The ring on our finger offers some reassurance that we're lovable, but this sentiment doesn't last for long. What we don't understand is that nothing outside of us can ever *make* us feel good . . . it's something we have to make happen all by ourselves.

Naturally, if you have plenty of friends, close relationships with your relatives, terrific neighbors in your community, and a loving and kind romantic partner, it's much easier to feel loved and supported than if you don't have all those people in your life. But if you're feeling bad despite being surrounded by those who care about you, it's time to stop looking for the one person who will whisk you away to a happy life. You need to start creating some healthier thoughts and more positive emotions.

In my 20s, I didn't go for long stretches between relationships. I was still holding on to the idea that the perfect man could be my knight in shining armor. Although I didn't recognize it at the time, I was holding back by being suspicious and jealous. When my distrust and emotional withholding affected the partnership to the point that it was on the rocks, I'd end it. After having been dumped once, I sure wasn't going to go through that again! I thought I'd minimize my suffering if I was the one to break off the romance, but that strategy never quite worked. I'd feel sad and empty after the relationship ended, then perk up when I met the next supposed Mr. Right. I'd commit to being his girlfriend, emotionally withdraw, become jealous . . . and then start the whole pattern over again.

I didn't realize I had the power within me to address the underlying issues that kept me perpetually on the lookout for a man to make me feel good about myself.

I was too busy focusing on my flaws and hoping to be rescued.

The Perfect Parachute

Back in the 1980s, women, who had never been in the workforce in great numbers, started to dream about having careers. We didn't want to simply get a job; we wanted to be fulfilled by our work and feel a sense of independence and competence. We were very eager to go out there and prove that we were capable of doing everything a man could. We believed that we, too, could find the winning formula to life, and a great position in a good company seemed to be a good start. Like many people, I read books like *What Color Is Your Parachute?* and strategized on how to create the perfect profession that would free me from feelings of powerlessness and unhappiness.

We ladies probably should have stopped and listened to the men who were warning us that not every job opportunity leads to a great career, that it takes a lot of hard work and perseverance to get ahead, and that if we *do* get ahead, we'll find that even the greatest occupation has its flaws. As many women did at the time, I idealized work. I enjoyed having my own money and had a strong work ethic. Success helped me feel better about myself, and since one good job easily led to another, I had high hopes for career fulfillment. Yet while I did like what I was doing, I soon learned that no job could rescue me from low self-esteem or a sense of lack.

Too many people become workaholics, sacrificing all their personal goals—from having a close-knit family

to setting aside time to give back to the community—because they're driven by a need to prove themselves worthy. The belief "I'm not good enough" keeps them going, but no matter how much money they make, how prestigious their title is, or how many accolades they receive, they still feel sad and inadequate.

Then there are those folks who find that their insecurities prevent them from flourishing in their careers: They don't get the promotion they want, and instead of looking honestly at themselves to determine what they might do differently, they just start to feel worse about themselves. They, too, long for that one perfect answer and think that if only they could turn their careers around, they'd stop feeling sad, jealous, and frustrated, and start seeing themselves as winners.

These days, I'm an entrepreneur, helping authors and experts reach their goals using Internet-marketing techniques. I've noticed that some of my clients who take my courses have completely unrealistic expectations of success. They hope that becoming a best-selling author will alleviate their painful feelings of inadequacy—but they don't want to do the work. Many aspiring writers want to spread the message of their book, but more than that, they want to be saved, and look to bestseller-dom to rescue them from a sense of failure. They don't realize that the only way to get rid of that outlook is to start *living* success regardless of what's happening to them. To become a winner, they must first *feel* like one.

Each of us has the power to change our emotions and create the feelings that will fuel our dreams. If we feel successful, we can create success; but if we don't, we won't be able to make our careers work for us.

Too many times we look to our professions to save us because we figure that with success comes money, and if we have enough money, our problems should go away.

Greenbacks to the Rescue

I've been rich *and* poor, and I'm not going to lie and say I wish I were poor again! Money is energy, and if used wisely, it can make life better in many ways. For example, when my mother became terminally ill, the pain I felt at the thought of losing her was intense. Yet having the financial resources to take considerable time off from work and spend many hours with her made the situation more bearable. I was deeply grateful for the resources I had. But like many people, at one point in my life I figured that money was the answer to every problem, that it would make all my suffering magically disappear.

My friend Anick likes to say, "If everyone hung their problems on a line the way they do their clothes, we'd all be quickly running to our own backyards." When I was a personal coach, I had clients who were struggling with some of the most difficult circumstances—from cheating spouses to terribly sick children to overwhelming financial problems—yet many of these people lived in lovely homes with meticulously landscaped lawns.

Success can also bring with it new responsibilities and stresses that some folks just aren't ready for. They may discover that some of their closest friends and relatives are jealous and feel entitled to some of their newfound wealth, or, despite feeling burned out and in need of a change, they might feel the pressure to keep their businesses going

because their employees are counting on them. At the same time, the problems they had before don't necessarily get fixed by an influx of money—and may even become more complicated when they receive it.

Of course, having little or no funds can be extremely stressful, too. A hefty bankroll or a solid stock portfolio can seem like the perfect liberator. Many people obsess about all they could do if only they had money, and don't think about what they could do *right now* to make the situation better.

When you focus on what you lack and don't maintain an abundance mentality, money usually doesn't come. If it does, it brings other problems along with it. Once again, to solve financial problems, you have to first create positive beliefs inside of you regardless of your circumstances. You have to *feel* rich to *become* rich.

What I think most men and women want, although they don't realize it, isn't to be wealthy, but to have enough money to achieve their goals and feel content instead of stressed or worried. Yet anyone can experience positive emotions regardless of how much cash they have! Money seems to be a terrific quick fix, but the more people understand true abundance and embrace what their hearts value most, the less they'll work themselves up about it . . . and the less likely they are to see it as having the power to rescue them.

From Passivity to Action

When the things you hoped would save you—people, success, or money—don't materialize, you're likely to become disillusioned and pessimistic. Even if they do

show up in your life, and you think, *Woo-hoo! I've been rescued!* you're building your happiness on a false foundation. The bottom can fall out at any time because real happiness is something that you have to create regardless of your circumstances. Release from your suffering is not the be-all and end-all you're looking for. It turns out that you, and only you, can change your emotional state and then begin to attract and manifest circumstances that mirror your new, more positive feelings. Working with the universe, you are your own rescuer.

Back in the 1980s, I first heard of self-help guru Louise Hay, who actually cured herself of cancer. She realized that the doctors weren't going to save her and began to focus on changing the thought patterns that she believed had caused her to become ill. Healing her emotions, she healed her body. I was amazed by her story and realized for the first time that maybe I, too, could begin to heal myself and end my suffering on my own.

Me, to the Rescue!

To become your own liberator, you must look at your role in creating the circumstances that make it difficult for you to be happy. Without judging yourself harshly or coming up with justifications for your feelings, simply notice what can be changed in your world. For example, you can alter your emotions, thoughts, attitudes, and behaviors. When you do, the people in your life will start to shift. If you're sick and stop looking to your doctor to rescue you and begin to support yourself, educate yourself about your illness, and address any underlying emotional patterns that may be creating or worsening your condition, then he or she will be better able to help you.

Don't just look to your romantic partner to make you happy. Create joyousness on your own, which will adjust the dynamic between the two of you and take the pressure of trying to fix your problems off him or her. Your partner will then find it easier to relax and create feelings of happiness rather than inadequacy, and you'll notice that he or she has more to give you emotionally.

We have the ability to create the circumstances of our lives. We don't have complete control over *everything,* but we also aren't as powerless as we may think. If we're looking for someone to do the work of changing our lives for us, trust me, it's not going to happen. We've got to rescue ourselves.

If you're not getting the results you want and have stopped looking for answers, if you've stalled out in your life and are feeling impatient—thinking you've gotten a raw deal in life—then you may be buying into the false idea that being rescued is the answer. There's a fine line between having *faith* that someone or something will show up in your life to help you and *expecting* that to happen.

Sometimes we fall into the trap of waiting to be saved because we're tired, afraid that we don't know how to solve our own issues . . . but we don't have to. It's not necessary to have any clue how to achieve what we want for ourselves. All we need to be aware of is what we desire and then create the feelings we'd have if we attained it, envisioning ourselves in the ideal situation and relishing every moment of it as it plays out in our imaginations. As we create confidence, joy, tranquility, and gratitude, we change our energy, and the forces in our corners of reality start to manifest and attract circumstances that match up with our new, positive states.

Unfortunately, the dream of being saved by someone or something will often prevent us from committing to help ourselves. Perhaps we believe deep down that if someone were to swoop in and give us the answers we need, it would prove that we're lovable and worthy of being saved . . . that's certainly how I felt when I was much younger. But this Cinderella-like dream, of being whisked away by someone and suddenly recognized as worthy and important, keeps us from discovering our own sense of self-worth and finding the means to solve problems and create a happy, fulfilling life.

Frustrated by not being rescued, we can become so desperate for that quick fix that we jump into a job or relationship, or make a sudden move in the hopes that it will be the one thing that solves everything and makes us winners at last. Inevitably, we end up with just as many problems, often the same ones we had before. A new situation looks like the old one because we haven't changed. As the saying goes: "Wherever you go, there you are." Our circumstances will always reflect what's happening inside of us.

So if finding a rescuer isn't the one thing, what is? For several years, I went to lectures, read books, and attended workshops to find out. I came to the conclusion that the one thing that was going to change my life forever was managing my thoughts. . . .

Chapter Two

THINK IT, BE IT

"When your mind thinks correctly, when
you understand the truth, when the thoughts
deposited in your subconscious mind are constructive,
harmonious, and peaceful, the magic working
power of your subconscious will respond and
bring about harmonious conditions, agreeable
surroundings, and the best of everything."

— FROM *THE POWER OF YOUR SUBCONSCIOUS MIND,*
BY DR. JOSEPH MURPHY

After I realized that I was the only one who was
going to rescue myself from my prison of sadness—and
that, in fact, I was the one who had locked myself in the
cell—I experienced a revelation. That day, in the 1980s,
I heard my mentor, Bob Proctor, speak about the power

of the mind. Essentially, he said that if you change your thoughts, you can change your life. *This must be it!* I thought.

The Power of Managing Your Thoughts

What Bob was talking about was completely new to me. I'd never been taught to be introspective, so I never gave much attention to the ideas in my head or stopped to consider whether they were serving me or holding me back.

I had a lot of things going on in my brain, and I began to go on long walks to explore them and started to jot them down in a journal. I also read several books on the importance of concentrating on my thoughts, such as *As a Man Thinketh* by James Allen and *The Power of Your Subconscious Mind* by Dr. Joseph Murphy. I came to understand how important it was to observe my thought patterns and notice whether they were positive and productive or negative and destructive. Were they the seeds that would help me achieve the life I desired? Or were they the beginning of sorrowful, resentful, or angry feelings?

One thing I noticed was that when I did discover an adverse thought (and I had a lot of them!), I'd immediately experience guilt and sadness over it. It took me a while to see that if I was going to feel bad about myself in this process of self-examination, then it was going to be pretty difficult to maintain my commitment to introspection. I decided that instead of judging my thoughts, I'd simply observe them unemotionally, like Sgt. Joe Friday on the old TV show *Dragnet:* in his suit and tie, notebook in hand, and expressionless face under his fedora, he'd say, "Just the facts, ma'am." I made a point of noting "just the facts" and stopped myself from generating ideas that would lead to more disempowering emotions.

Because I'd been setting aside time to explore my mental activity, I started being more aware of it in everyday situations. As I was driving or reading my mail, I'd notice things that would come into my mind, and I'd wonder, *Is that going to get me closer to my goals?* Before, a thought such as *Ugh, I'm running late, I should have left the house earlier; I'm such an idiot* would have popped into my mind and made me feel ashamed as I created the opinion that I was being foolish or incompetent. Now that I was becoming more aware, I tended to stop myself from focusing on a string of thoughts that matched my feelings of panic about being late for work and my overall unworthiness. Instead, I'd reason with myself, *Okay, I may be a little late, but I can't change that at this moment— I'll simply do the best I can with the time I have. The lesson here is to start getting ready earlier or ignore the telephone if it rings as I'm heading out the door.* I could identify ways to see the situation as a learning experience because I wasn't stuck in the drama of writing an internal monologue about why I should feel awful.

The other thing that examining what was in my head taught me was that there were solid reasons for why I wasn't achieving the results I was seeking—namely, many of my views were downright toxic! It's amazing how many detrimental thoughts one person can come up with in a short period of time. I looked at my unsatisfying relationships (which never quite worked out), my problems at my job, and my financial struggles, and started pondering, *What sorts of beliefs about men, work, and money are leading to these results, which are not the ones I want?* Needless to say, what I'd been telling myself wasn't exactly positive and affirming! What a revelation!

Discovering the quality of your thoughts is very important, because after being the calm observer, you can switch into the role of impartial judge and ask yourself this simple question: *Is this a thought that will lead me toward happiness and success or away from it?* If it isn't working for you, make the choice to banish it from your mind. It may appear again, but remembering the decision you've made, you can counter it with: *I don't believe that anymore.* The more you reject those unproductive, negative sentiments, the less they'll arise.

How Thoughts and Emotions Get Wrapped Around Each Other

Why are negative thoughts so destructive? Because their power is in the emotions they create, which we hold on to so tightly. Some musings could be seen as neutral, such as *I'm running late* or *My friend didn't call me like he said he would.* However, once we start to embellish them, we usually create negative perceptions that wind around them and cause us to suffer. For example:

Neutral thought	Embellished, negative thought	Negative emotions
"I'm running late."	"I'm always late. What's wrong with me anyway?"	Shame, embarrassment
"My friend didn't call me like he said he would."	"He must not like me." or "He's self-centered and rude. He doesn't care about my feelings!"	Worthlessness, embarrassment, humiliation or Anger, resentment

When you analyze your negative thoughts, you can see not only how they make you feel bad, but how distorted they are as well. It may *feel* as if you're *always* late, but that may not actually be true (if it is, you have to look at why you're not leaving enough time to get your tasks done). Thinking *I'm always messing up somehow* will feed any sentiments of inadequacy you have. If a friend doesn't call you as promised, there could be any number of reasons, so it's a distortion to think it simply *has* to be that he doesn't like you or care about your feelings. You can't weigh the evidence of whether something is literally true or not when you can't see past your reality. Being an observer allows you to temporarily set aside your emotions so that you can be objective about what's really going on.

The more you look at your thoughts, the more you'll realize the importance of their energy. Notice the quality and intensity of the sentiments wrapped around them. If you want to replace your unproductive attitude with a productive one, you'll have to pay attention to the energy you're attaching to it. For example, if you're insisting to yourself, *I'm happy that I'm making a million dollars this year!* that can be an excellent assertion. However, if you're embellishing this particular statement with a negative new thought such as *I don't really believe this; it's an unrealistic goal,* then you won't be affirming your belief that you can achieve the goal. Instead, you'll be stressing your lack and insecurity, which will produce results you don't like. To manifest a million dollars, you have to *feel like a million dollars!* You have to perceive a powerful sense of abundance, enthusiasm, worthiness, and confidence. If the statement "I'm happy I'm making huge amounts of money this year!" makes you feel a greater sense of passion and prosperity, then use it as your affirmation instead of "I'm happy I'm making a million dollars this year!"

Everyone is different. A declaration that makes someone feel unambiguously confident might make you feel unsure, and vice versa, so choose the one that works for you. You'll find that if you attach enough powerful, positive emotions to your affirmations over a period of time, you'll believe them.

To fuel our beliefs, we need to be aware of the language we're using. Thoughts such as *I am making a million dollars and my bank account is full of cash! I am rich beyond my wildest dreams!* might make us feel excited, rich, and full of possibilities. These words help us envision our bank accounts with huge amounts of money in them, a stack of cash in our wallets, and a flood of checks from clients coming in. It doesn't matter if all of this isn't literally true at the moment, as long as the words, feelings, and images we create in our minds make us *feel* rich. Positive convictions propel us toward our goals and give us the magnetic ability to attract what we desire.

Soon after I discovered the importance of supporting my thoughts with the power of positive emotions, I began to see better results. But there was something else I had to learn about thoughts: sometimes they're unconscious, which can be far more forceful than conscious ones.

Those Secret Thoughts That Trip Us Up

All of us have subconscious thoughts. Sometimes they remain hidden in our minds because they're so painful that we don't want to think about them. They can also be ideas that we created or accepted long ago but that we no longer concern ourselves with. If they aren't serving us anymore yet we don't realize that they're holding us back, then they could be greatly influencing our emotions, behaviors, and conscious perceptions. Although these thoughts are hidden away from our awareness, they're like a computer program that's constantly running and interfering with other ones. Just like a virus that keeps crashing our system and sabotaging our work, that negative program needs to be addressed, not ignored.

When you're having subconscious, destructive ideas, you may have an inkling that something is going on. The last time I had a computer virus, the little hourglass on my monitor spun and spun until I realized, *Uh-oh, this is taking too long—this isn't a good sign!* And then, of course, the program shut down. Subconscious thoughts can give you a twinge or a subtle feeling of discomfort. If you find the courage to admit being unsettled or uncomfortable, you can discover what these notions are, examine them, and decide whether you want to hold on to them.

When I feel out of sorts or slightly offended, irritated, frustrated, or sad, I stop myself and wonder, *What's going on here?* If for some reason I don't take that opportunity to analyze what's in my head at that moment, I come back to it later when I'm journaling before bedtime and explore what I avoided earlier. I always remember that just like everyone, I'll have my moments when I need to examine my conscious and subconscious reflections, notice their qualities and intensity, and, if they're negative, decide what I'd like to replace them with.

Acting with Exuberance

As I explained, thoughts are powerful because they're the fuel of our emotions, and this fuel propels the vehicle, generating action. If we truly feel that we're deserving of a loving, committed soul mate—and we allow ourselves to experience and savor how fantastic it is to be adored and cherished—we'll find ourselves enthusiastic about meeting new potential partners and go out there and do it with exuberance!

When people tell me, "I'd like to find someone, but I hate dating," I know it's because they're holding on to negative assumptions about their prospects, or about what dating will be like, based on past experiences of low self-esteem. They claim that they want to find a partner, but then they come up with all sorts of excuses for not going out with new people. They're afraid they won't meet that special person, and then they'll feel even worse.

Once you create a positive thought, infuse it with the emotions to match. Actually visualize what you want and sense how fantastic it feels to be achieving it in your imagination. Act *as if* you have what you want, create how you'd feel if you had it, and think, *It is mine already!*

Believe that positive thought, feel that marvelous feeling, and let yourself rise up out of your sadness and go forward with gusto. You'll find that you're inspired to follow through with action even when you meet obstacles.

Recently I consulted with an author who was frustrated that after a month of trying to procure campaign partners for a viral marketing drive to sell his book, he only had a few people who were willing to be a part of his plan. "I don't understand why I'm not seeing results," he shared, right before he told me why he wouldn't be able to achieve his goals and vented about all the problems he'd encountered so far.

Now, I couldn't help thinking about another client I was working with, who was planning the same type of marketing campaign and had started trying to find partners at about the same time . . . only she'd already found ten times as many as he had. Every time I talked to her, she was brimming over with excitement about everyone she'd signed up so far and whom she was planning to approach—and I felt that her book had a less exciting and fresh topic than his did! I was certain that the problem wasn't with this man's product, but with his lack of hopeful emotional energy that would fuel the actions he needed to take, infuse others with enthusiasm, and ultimately attract them to help market his book. I knew he needed to understand that feeling and thinking optimistically leads to positive actions and results.

"I swear," my unhappy client assured me, "I'll go bankrupt if necessary to meet my goal. It's that important to me!"

I told him I didn't think that was the most helpful attitude to have. "What I suggest," I said, "is that you focus on being passionate and persistent and having fun. After all, you're enthusiastic about your book and

your topic, right? Feel that excitement swelling up in you and then make the next phone call. Your joy will be infectious, and I think you're going to see much better results."

He told me he'd give it a try—maybe he *had* been too insecure, and it had been evident in his voice when he'd talked to potential partners. Sure enough, a week later, he'd quadrupled his numbers.

Positive thoughts and feelings also open up the creative floodgates, leading to actions that are innovative and which capture people's attention. For example, one person who came to see me baked 1,500 cookies for potential clients, decorating each one by hand. This was one of several steps she took that eventually led to a seven-figure advance for a self-published novel, which is an extraordinary amount of money for a first-time author. Baking the cookies wasn't a gigantic sacrifice for her, but it was a clever idea that came out of her passion for her book. She was able to see the resources she had—which included a good oven but not a hefty bank account!—and use them to her advantage. All sorts of options are open to each one of us when we think, feel, and act in positive ways!

Of course, we can't literally do *anything* if we put our minds to it. None of us can think our way into sprouting wings and flying or single-handedly creating world peace; but if we understand the connection between subconscious thoughts, conscious thoughts, emotions, and actions, we can do *just about* anything.

Discovering that you're the one who holds the key to unlock the prison of your unhappiness is empowering. But to free yourself, you have to be able to tolerate the discomfort of discovering that you've been your own jailer.

It's hard to admit a mistake, but don't think that you should judge yourself for having unproductive thoughts and feelings you avoided examining. It's human nature to try to steer clear of pain; however, once you recognize that the best way to do so is to be uncomfortable for a little while as you scrutinize what your thoughts, feelings, and actions have been, you liberate yourself from unnecessary suffering. You can actually move forward into creating the life you want for yourself.

Banishing Brain Blips

Once you've done the difficult but important work of uncovering your destructive and unproductive thoughts and feelings, you can change them. You do this by actually replacing them with something better.

Although it was painful for me to face my core belief that I was undeserving of love and success, once I did, I forgave myself for holding on to such a poisonous assumption that had led to much suffering in my life. I knew that my job was to replace this thought with the simple, empowering conviction: *I am deserving and worthy of love and success.* I had to believe it and feel it, and it was helpful to think of myself as one of God's creatures deserving of the pleasures this world has to offer. I'm not more entitled to love and success than the next person, but like everyone, I *am* entitled to these things.

Every day I would repeat this affirmation to myself and fully feel it. In the same way I brushed my teeth each morning, I attended to my *mental* hygiene. Not a day went by where I didn't spend time thinking and truly believing: *I am deserving and worthy of love and success.* If

No, you're not! popped into my head, I recognized it for what it was: a *brain blip*—a thought randomly generated by the wiring in my brain that matched up with my old, destructive belief system. I didn't give these brain blips any more time or energy; I just saw them for what they were—beliefs that I no longer wanted to waste my time with. I banished them as I focused harder on creating this wonderful, enriching view: *I am deserving and worthy of love and success.* (My book *Your Destiny Switch* explains many of the techniques I've discovered that help us switch out of negativity and into positive thinking and feeling.)

Carrying on as if you've already accomplished your goal is crucial to helping you get where you want to go, but you should also take advantage of *all* the opportunities for spontaneously switching to positive, productive sentiments. In the old days, when I was caught up in negativity, I'd witness a man go up to his girlfriend, put his arms around her and kiss her, and I'd think, *I don't have that.* I'd generate sadness and lack in my mind and start embellishing the core belief *I am undeserving* with an inner dialogue that made me feel even worse. Now I know that a much better response to a situation like this—which used to bring up old beliefs about unworthiness —is not to embellish that brain blip when it comes up, but to instead consciously assert to myself, *Isn't that beautiful? There's so much love in the world. I'm deserving of it, too! I'm so glad I have love in my life!* I came to realize that feeling appreciative of the love of my family and friends actually drew romance to me and caused me to act in amorous ways . . . which made me even more attractive to men!

You can apply the same technique to anything you desire. To achieve wealth and abundance, don't linger in thoughts about debt or financial challenges. Be grateful for the luxuries you have. Truly relish the feeling of prosperity you experience as you look at the stately homes in the affluent part of town. Be thankful for the successes you've had and allow yourself to feel complete confidence that you'll build upon them. Be proud of the marvelous talents and skills you possess, which can be used to help you create and attract more of what you want. When you find yourself feeling jealous of someone who seems to have more than you, don't start generating the thought *I shouldn't be jealous . . . how awful of me!* Simply recognize the brain blip for what it is, banish it, and use this opportunity to ask yourself, *What makes me think I can't have that?* After all, jealousy is based in the belief that someone else has something you can't have.

Explore what your hidden judgment is, and replace it with something more optimistic. Then wonder, *What would I like to feel instead of jealousy?* Create that emotion and a positive, matching sentiment that will bring you closer to what you desire for yourself.

If all of this sounds too easy, believe me, I know how hard it can be to trust that we have the power to manage our thoughts and emotions. In my younger years, I had boyfriends tell me I was "too sensitive" or that I "should have thicker skin" (I don't handle teasing well at all). I figured that there were individuals who were tough and resilient, and others, like me, whose emotions were more intense or painful . . . and that people like me couldn't do much to change how we feel. Now I know that everyone can use specific techniques for changing their thoughts and feelings, and reinforce the new, healthier ones they want to experience.

Making these changes does take time and effort, and the old feelings can still crop up at times. Not long ago,

my late mother was very weak from cancer and lying in a hospital bed. My brother and I were trying to figure out how we might get her outside on a lovely day so that she could enjoy the sunshine and be in touch with nature. Mom was getting a little agitated, saying, "Don't be silly. I can't go outside!" My brother had the idea to roll her bed, which was on wheels, down the corridors and out the door to the hospital's grassy courtyard. I was saying something about how maybe Mom could transfer into a wheelchair when my mother emphatically said, "I just can't stand Peggy!"

In an instant, all of my feelings of being unworthy rushed to the surface, and tears welled up in my eyes. I felt all the pain of my childhood—when it seemed I just couldn't please my parents—coming back to me. *My mother can't stand me*—what a painful thought! I turned away so that my brother and mother couldn't see the expression on my face or the tears that were threatening to roll down my cheeks.

"Yeah, Peggy. Mom's right. She can't stand, so we're going to have to forget about the wheelchair and just try moving the bed," my brother said, totally unaware of how upset I was.

"Yes, let's move the bed," my mom said plainly.

It was then that I realized what had just happened. My old feeling of inadequacy had distorted what I'd heard. What my weak and fragile mother had really said was, "I just *can't stand,* Peggy." I'd missed the comma! As I realized my mistake, I started to laugh.

"What's so funny?" my brother asked.

"I'll explain later," I said, cheering up.

It was a powerful reminder of just how strong old programming can be!

By managing our thoughts, and the feelings that we wrap around them, we can escape the prison of our own making. We don't have to be the people we are today. Too often we take security in predictability and convince ourselves that since we've always been anxious or unhappy, had to struggle financially, or been without a romantic partner, that's how our lives will be. We live in a town called Misery but think it's a town called Honesty. We create our reality. If we want to believe that our existence can be deeply fulfilling and joyous, we have the ability to manifest that—starting today.

The day you switch your perspective and recognize your power to change your life, you'll be amazed by how much more hopeful you'll feel. Awareness is like a staircase: each step brings you up one more level, and the farther you ascend, the more you can see.

Your thoughts are limited by your perspective. Widen it, and it will be easier to recognize when your thoughts are holding you back . . . and new ones that make you feel more pleasant will appear.

Discovering my ability to control my disposition was an extremely important step in my self-growth, but I came to understand that managing my thoughts isn't the ultimate answer for life—the one thing. I was still unhappy and feeling a lack of purpose. I was searching for something more, not just relief from suffering, but something that would be the key to true fulfillment. That's when I discovered the power of *goals*.

Chapter Three

GOOOOOAAAAALLLLL!

> *"Set a goal to achieve something that is so big, so exhilarating, that it excites you and scares you at the same time. It must be a goal that is so appealing, so much in line with your spiritual core, that you can't get it out of your mind. If you don't get chills when you set a goal, you're not setting big enough goals."*
>
> — BOB PROCTOR

Examining my thoughts made me realize that there was a connection between what I was thinking, feeling, and doing, and the results I was achieving. Once I recognized that I actually had the power to change my thoughts and emotions, I got very excited. I felt

unstoppable! Instead of focusing so much on my prob-lems, I started envisioning what I wanted for myself and making new goals.

I'd always been motivated by concrete objectives: to make enough money to afford my first apartment and car; and to find the man of my dreams, get married, and start a family. I felt that if I could reach these goals, I'd be happy.

Not everyone is goal oriented, and that's okay. To paraphrase motivational speaker and author Og Man-dino, if we're happy with life the way it is and aren't actively pursuing something better, there's nothing wrong with that. But we're all creative beings by nature. If we're not working toward coming up with something new, then we feel the urge to bring about more of what we have that's giving us pleasure: more quality time with the people we love, more comfort, more time to pursue our hobbies, and so on. My feeling is, why should we settle for very good when we can put forth some effort and make our lives fantastic? We can set simple goals for improving our existence, such as spending more time engaging in family activities, learning something new, meeting new people, or trying out-of-the-ordinary pur-suits to keep a sense of excitement and adventure.

Whatever our goals are—and however modest or grand they are—it's understandable that we want to see them manifest exactly as we imagined. Our passion inspires us to ponder all the marvelous details of how we might get from here to there. As we pass each road marker, we feel more confident that we'll achieve our desires as planned. But if that sign doesn't show up when expected, or we realize that we may have made a wrong turn or are facing an obstacle, our hopes can fizzle. As I learned about goals, I came to realize that the best way to attain them without losing hope is to truly understand how to set and work with those that are achievable.

The key is knowing that not every goal is right for *you*. The better aligned with your inner passion an objective is, the more likely it will be that you'll see excellent results.

Desires from the Heart

If you set a concrete goal, a marker of success, it can keep you focused on what you want to create. However, if you don't establish that benchmark, you might start generating negative thoughts and feelings. Determination and single-mindedness can be very helpful for achieving your ambitions, but at the same time, you have to accept that the universe has its own ideas about how to make your dreams a reality.

Too often we set standards for success without examining the beliefs that underlie our aspirations. If we were to look more closely at our most heartfelt desires, we might wish for something different. For example, when I was working as a goal-achievement coach, almost all of my clients set an objective of making more money. Sometimes they'd want to make a specific amount by a certain time, such as a six-figure salary within two years. The problem with such a goal is that it's limiting. Why not a seven-figure salary? Why within two years—what if you could achieve it in six months? What if the money could come to you not through salary or by working more hours at your job, but from investments or simply through the abundance of the universe? I'm

not saying that the best option is to buy lottery tickets and cross your fingers, but time and time again, I've seen people who trust that the universe will help them co-create wealth go on to receive unexpected large amounts of money—from the government, an inheritance, or a long-forgotten bank account. When we try to dictate *how* and *when* our goal manifests, we restrict ourselves.

It's also important that you understand that to make any goal become a reality, it must be fueled by passion. If it's out of sync with your heart's desire, you may get stuck in the feeling that you're like Sisyphus, the mythological figure who was continually rolling a rock up the hill, only to have to start all over again as soon as it rolled down to the bottom. But if your aim is rooted in your deepest passion, you could be performing the most mundane or difficult task and you'll still feel enthusiastic.

Sometimes you think that you're excited about a goal, but then one day when you're cold-calling, driving long distances to see clients, or dealing with a grumpy partner, you'll say to yourself, "This is no fun. What was I thinking?" If the goal was always rooted in passion, you'll be able to switch into a more positive mode and push through the obstacle . . . or find a way around it and get back to the joy and enthusiasm you initially felt for it. The hard work along the way, as well as the experience of having overcome roadblocks, can make reaching that pinnacle all the more fulfilling and rewarding. However, if the conviction wasn't there to begin with, you'll sputter out quickly.

When thinking about your goals, get in touch with your deepest beliefs about them. Take some time to truly examine your objectives before you focus on how to achieve them. For example, most people will readily say,

"I'd like to get rich so that I can be free from financial burdens and have plenty of money!" I think there's a great benefit in exploring what's driving those desires. Are your underlying motivations positive and empowering or negative and disempowering? For instance, if the secret thought that's connected to that goal is this: *I'd like to be free from financial burdens and have plenty of money so that I can win my father's approval at last and feel like a success because I don't feel good about myself,* then ouch! That's a belief that you need to replace. You may decide to set the same monetary goal, but with a more positive belief supporting it, such as: *I'd like to be free from financial burdens and have plenty of wealth because I'd love to be able to do more for myself and my family.* This, in turn, can become the affirmation: *I have plenty of wealth to do all that I want for myself and my family.*

When you switch your thoughts and feelings to more positive ones, your goals may change. You may discover that you really don't need a lot of money. Maybe your genuine passion is simply to have the financial freedom to do what matters most to you at this stage in your life—which could be traveling, or having a job where you really enjoy work and feel that you're part of a team that's making a difference in the world. And, as long as you've got enough money to focus more on your dream than on making ends meet, that would be enough for you.

Let's say your goal is rooted in a positive and empowering thought. First, express it in the present tense so as not to communicate to the universe that you want something or are creating a feeling of lack. You might word your goal in this way: *I have a wonderful romantic partner and a circle of supportive, loving friends in my community;* or *I enjoy creating a product that helps those in my*

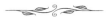
field do their job more efficiently, which allows us to focus on the most important aspects of our work.

Next, explore your thoughts and feelings further in order to clarify your ambitions and give yourself some ideas on how to get started. You'll begin by researching, learning, and exploring—finding resources for more information and support. At this early stage, you'll most likely be in touch with your enthusiasm, and any obstacles that you become aware of—such as warnings from people that your goal may be difficult to achieve or the revelation that you have a lot of work ahead of you—will probably seem like those you can overcome. If you find that you've had to sacrifice and even experience emotional discomfort, fatigue, and frustration after you've been pursuing your goal, you'll realize just how important it is to stay in touch with your passion—because it's the fuel that can propel you forward when situations are difficult.

Tapping into the Power of Your Passion

I use techniques every day for reconnecting to my excitement and enthusiasm, which help me generate feelings of curiosity, confidence, faith, joy, and love. For example, I like to work with a *goal card:* a simple index card on which I've written down my objectives in the areas of personal and spiritual development, relationships, finances, business and career, and health. You may be content with your overall life and feel a strong urge to change only in one area, and that's fine—if so, your goal card may simply have that one important aim written on it. Look at your goal card as often as you can, reading

it with great feeling as you reconnect to your passion.

I work with men and women whose goals are based on passion, but I've certainly met people who, when they examine their aspirations, discover that these intentions aren't rooted in what they desire but in what they think they *should* desire. If you have to talk yourself into pursuing a particular goal, you'll probably find yourself alphabetizing your spice rack and reading every advertisement that comes in the mail before you make one phone call to help you attain what you say you want! Don't feel bad about your elaborate ways of avoiding what you think you should do; be gentle with yourself. If your heart isn't in it, you're not going to make it happen. Let go of anything that's rooted in negative beliefs and emotions; instead, tap into the power of your passion and let it help you determine what you want to achieve.

The good news is that you don't even have to know how to accomplish what your heart is set on. You simply have to know what it is, focus on it, and create the feelings and thoughts to support it. Actually experience the emotions you'd feel as if you'd already reached your goal, and the path will reveal itself in proper time. Start with passion—you'll know just what actions to take.

Are You Truly Ready for Success?

You may be a bit unclear about what you really want for yourself. If you don't research and consider what achieving a particular goal will entail, you might end up feeling dissatisfied or disappointed once you accomplish what you set out to do. Imagining that you've already

made it to the top of the mountain and achieved success not only helps you create the powerful emotions that propel you forward on your journey, but also prepares you for certain aspects of this fulfilled objective that you might not have considered.

I sometimes see this with writers who want to become best-selling authors. They know they want to make money, get their ideas out into the world, and help people, and these are all wonderful objectives that come from passion and positive beliefs and emotions. However, every situation has its challenges. I achieved my goal of writing a bestseller, but quickly became overwhelmed by all the demands that came with it. Every time I checked my e-mail, my inbox was full. The media was constantly calling for interviews, and I did so many that I found myself on live radio saying something while feeling a little stressed out and worrying, *Uh-oh, did I just say that five minutes ago? Or was that something I said during my last interview?* People would make requests of me, and if I didn't answer their calls or e-mails quickly, they'd often write to me again or leave messages that were filled with disappointment and even a little anger. I remember once after a phenomenally successful day of Internet marketing, I was overjoyed with what I'd achieved and started rapidly reading through the hundreds of e-mails I'd just received. Suddenly, I came across one that simply said, "This is a joke and so are you." It was so hurtful that I still remember the exact wording now, eight years later!

Momentarily, this virtual punch to the gut caused me to spin a series of thoughts that created more pain, but I knew enough about mind management by then to insist to myself, *Okay, this fellow has a problem if he's so mean to me—my intent to help others only comes from a place of joy, love, and a genuine desire to lift people up,* and I let go of that ugly feeling. But the surprise attack made me realize that since I'd put myself out there, there would be people who, because of their own problems, would lash out at me. That was part of being in the public eye that I hadn't considered. I know I can't possibly please everyone and meet their expectations; however, I've learned how to do the best I can so that at the end of the day, I'm able to let go of the demands on me and feel good about what I've accomplished.

Whatever your goal, expect at least some surprises once you reach it. Learn what you can from people who have been there, as they can let you in on the more unsettling concerns you hadn't thought about. If someone is very pessimistic or discouraging, recognize that they may have unresolved issues of their own that would cause them to be discouraging about *any* goal and negative about *any* situation.

Years ago, a friend of mine named Jan was very excited about moving to New York City and becoming an actress, and she shared this goal with someone who had lived and worked there in the past. "You'll only be able to afford to live with roommates in Brooklyn, Queens, or New Jersey," the woman warned. Jan said she knew that and was looking forward to finding an apartment outside of Manhattan. "And you'll have to take the subways," the woman warned. "You'll be crushed up against other people for at least 20 minutes every morning and every night when you take it to and from work." Jan was still undeterred, but the woman's list of horrors of living on a budget in New York City was endless. Finally, Jan pleasantly ended the conversation. Later, when she related this story to me, it was clear that she wasn't upset by it,

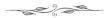
but she did admit it was good to know what she was in for so there wouldn't be as many unpleasant surprises. Finally she commented, "I think that this poor woman would probably have been miserable riding a private jet to the world's best spa for a weekend of pampering!"

When receiving advice, listen to what the other person has to say even if you disagree. Be respectful; thoughtfully take in their perspective and mull it over yourself. You might run into those with issues that taint their point of view and advice, or you could even find that the people you're approaching are brusque or arrogant for reasons of their own. If you choose not to create detrimental emotions in response to their behavior, you can take what they say that's of value and discard the rest—and then look around for others who can offer support in a more positive way.

Whether it's sharing a small bathroom with your very first roommate as a young person or putting up with your partner's moods in a long-term relationship, there are always challenges in attaining your goals. Remember, what may be a drawback for one person could be a plus for you. By doing some research on those who've already attained what you want to achieve, you can learn how to cope with an increased workload, reduced privacy or flexibility, or greater responsibilities. Most important, if your aim is right for you and rooted in your passion, you'll be able to handle these changes without giving in to negative feelings and thoughts.

Readying yourself for success also means letting go of what might be holding you back. Arielle Ford, author of *The Soulmate Secret,* says that if you really want a long-term, committed, loving relationship, you have to clean out your closets—literally! You must make room in your life for something new to come in. Let go of your distractions, and prepare the nest for your success.

More Than Just "Good Enough"

Life's greatest rewards won't be reaped by doing a "good enough" job. Think about the parent who takes the extra time to learn more about why her daughter is doing poorly at school—once she sets aside her embarrassment or frustration and digs deep, she might discover that her child has a learning disability that can be addressed. What a gift she's giving her daughter!

If you do what everyone else says can't be done because you're like a dog with a bone, utterly determined to reach your goal, you may be called "crazy" or "too intense." The road to success isn't always comfortable, and it can be lonely—and you may even start to think, *Maybe they're right and I am crazy.* At these moments, the best thing to do is reconnect to your passion. When you do, you'll regain your faith and even find yourself coming up with new, creative ideas for how to attain the goal. You might even figure out how to reach people in a new and exciting way to bring them on board for sharing your dream.

I have a friend who teaches yoga and was having difficulty attracting new clients to her class. People who were taking classes tended to sign up for sessions taught by the instructors they knew rather than trying someone they weren't familiar with. By offering some free classes to newcomers, she brought in students who discovered they really liked her methods. Another client of mine agreed to trade his professional services at

a greatly reduced fee to someone in exchange for public endorsement of his work if the customer was satisfied. Because the customer had nothing to lose, she agreed to work with my client and ending up giving him a terrific endorsement that helped him acquire new business.

Achieving goals always requires work. Even if you want to win the lottery, you still have to go out and buy the tickets! You may have to spend a considerable amount of time and money to get where you want to go; however, if you avoid thinking about what you're giving up and instead focus on your passion—generating feelings of joy, enthusiasm, and confidence—you'll probably find that the benefits you reap are so great that the sacrifices are definitely worth making.

Aiming to Be Number One vs.
Aiming to Achieve Your Personal Best

Years ago I remember watching heavyweight-boxing champion Muhammad Ali on television before a fight, exclaiming, "I'm the greatest!" It was his signature line. Some people felt he was being conceited, but I understood that when he was entering a competition, he needed to truly believe that he was the greatest boxer in the ring. What he believed, he achieved.

Creating an emotional state in which you feel that *you* are "the greatest" will allow you to meet any goal and reach your personal best. However, it's important not to be too literal in aiming to become number one. There are few things in life where there's a clear top dog or number one achiever. To be a champion in life, be the best that *you* can be. There's nothing wrong with healthy competition, but to be your best, you don't necessarily have to "best" anyone. It's not always true that someone has to lose for you to win—that's only the case in a sports competition or most types of games. When Muhammad Ali was declared the winner of a title, his opponent definitely lost and had to turn over the championship belt. But the belief *I have to be number one* is often rooted in feelings of scarcity—that if you don't come out on top, ahead of everyone else, you won't reap any rewards. There can only be one heavyweight champion of the world at a time, but there can be many top real-estate agents in your area, thousands of best-selling authors, and millions of top-notch parents. By discovering what you uniquely have to offer, you can be the best at what you do and achieve the results you desire.

A while back, I had a client who wanted to become highly successful at selling books and giving seminars. He worked very hard, believed in his message, and put in the extra work needed to market himself—he had his own Internet-radio program and newsletter and was continually looking for ways to advertise his products and services. However, he had a very strong competitive streak: whenever he looked around at his peers or at others who were doing similar work but achieving greater financial success, he'd come to me and complain, "I'm better than they are, so why are they doing so well?" It was as if he had his foot on the gas but his ego kept hitting the brakes. In fact, he even developed a stress-related illness that sidetracked him for many months. By constantly braking and accelerating, he was wasting fuel and burning out his engine. What he didn't understand was that if he'd been able to get excited about other people's success, his own would increase.

If we can be genuine about generating the emotions of joy, enthusiasm, and abundance within ourselves, the universe will work with us to bring about situations that match these feelings. Letting go of the destructive belief: *I can't reach my goal if someone else reaches his* opens us up to the more positive thought: *There's enough abundance in the world for everyone to share in it!*

What Is a "Realistic" Goal?

I believe in dreaming big. What makes a goal realistic is, of course, if it's possible in the physical world. If you're 49 and are thinking that you'd like to take up swimming with the intention of winning a gold medal in the 100-meter backstroke in the next Olympics, that's probably not going to happen! But beyond that, a realistic objective adheres to the following: (1) it's truly fueled by your internal passion; (2) you're willing to work hard at, and make sacrifices for it; and (3) it can manifest in more than one way. For example, if you take up swimming at age 49 and practice very hard, you may be able to find a competition for middle-aged people, compete in the backstroke event, and win! If you're creative and open to how your goal might manifest, you just may discover a route to achievement that you hadn't considered before.

You can ask the universe for anything, but the question is: are you willing to do what it takes to get what you want? While hard work and sacrifice are necessities for achieving any goal, never allow yourself to abandon your family, health, or well-being to attain it. If an ambition requires that sort of sacrifice, it's probably rooted in self-critical sentiments such as: *I'm not good enough unless I achieve something grand, I don't deserve to feel good unless I prove myself worthy,* or *I'm afraid of what will happen if I don't meet this goal.* If you're desperate or willing to give up everything to fulfill your goal, I hope you'll stop and take the time to explore what your true passion is and make sure you aren't being driven by any negative thoughts or feelings.

When I work with authors who want their books to be bestsellers, I ask them the following three questions to help them determine if their goals are realistic:

#1: Will Meeting Your Goal Fulfill a Need That People Have?

As an expert in Internet marketing, I've helped many authors learn how to sell their self-help and inspirational books. I believe that there will always be people who want to improve their lives, achieve their goals, and experience greater happiness and fulfillment—so there will always be an audience for these books. I also believe that people often need to hear a message many times and in many different ways before it sinks in, so even books that discuss topics that have already been written about can still sell well to some degree. However, sometimes a potential client will tell me he or she has written a book on a subject that appeals to a very limited audience, or I'll feel that it doesn't provide a fresh take on a concept. In that case, I'll suggest that the author do more research before pouring money, energy, and heart into writing, producing, and selling a book that there isn't a market for. Everyone wants to believe they've got

a best-selling idea, but some just aren't that strong.

When it comes to personal goals, our needs always overlap with those of others. If fulfilling our desires creates positive feelings in us, these sentiments will be created in others. Yet if our ambition is based on lack, attaining our objective may actually harm others.

Let's say your goal is to make a lot of money because you feel you don't have enough and don't care about bringing value to the world. In this case, you're likely to cut corners to save money and will provide an inferior product or service. Such an outcome doesn't benefit the world—it actually harms it—by giving consumers reasons to be distrustful and pessimistic. People are often reluctant to try new things because they've been burned before, which makes it hard for those coming out with good products to convince others that they can once again trust something they've never heard of.

If your desire is to help others and be a better person, citizen, parent, child, or employee yourself—helping fulfill the world's need for more love, generosity, and information—then reaching that goal will not only accomplish your personal aspirations, but it will also affect others positively and meet their needs. The more unconditional value you give to others, the more abundance you experience.

#2: Why Should People Trust, Support, and Listen to You?

I often ask my clients who want to write books some or all of the following questions: "What makes you an expert on this topic?" "What do you have to offer that's different?" "Do you have an unusual story to share that can bring attention to an important topic?" "Do you have a fresh way of looking at an old subject that will help others learn and grow?" and "Are you exceptionally empathetic or able to effectively teach people?"

Whatever your goal is, you'll need others to assist you in meeting it, so it's important to ask yourself these questions. You'll need to identify the unique gifts that will help you share information, resources, and support with others so that they can reciprocate. Give, and you will receive. When you recognize your own set of talents and personal perspectives—and appreciate them—you'll find ways to express them to the world in a positive and beneficial way, and then reap the benefits.

If you feel that you have nothing special to offer, then you'll find it difficult to feel good about yourself and maintain your passion as you work toward your goal, so do some digging.

#3: Do You Have the Resources You'll Need to Achieve Your Goal, or Are You Willing to Acquire Them?

Remember, you don't have to know how to get from where you are to your end goal, but you do have to be willing to work hard and not skip crucial steps. You also must have—or be willing and able to acquire— the resources you'll need, whether that might include enough capital and cash flow to start a business, good communication skills, or specialized knowledge.

Every objective requires learning new skills and honing ones you already have. You may need to have the

money to go back to school or purchase educational materials, or you may need emotional support to help you stay strong as you develop better parenting skills to deal with your child's difficult behavior. You may also need to learn coping skills so that you can find balance in your life and remain in a state of happiness as you're juggling work, raising kids, or taking care of an elderly parent. Sometimes, to acquire the resources you need, you'll have to come up with more money or time—and this means making sacrifices. As you consider your goal and what it requires, be honest with yourself about what you'll need to do and whether you truly are ready to make the required commitment.

Deciding on your goal requires careful consideration, in part because pursuing any goal will affect the people you care about. If you start a new business, you may not have as much time to spend supporting your friend who's going through a difficult divorce or coaching your child's sports team. If your ambition requires you to make a geographical move or to travel more and you have a family that needs you at home, you may have a conflict. By reconnecting with your deepest passion and remaining open to the many ways in which your goals might manifest, you'll have an easier time discovering the options that are available to you.

When defining your intent, consider the needs of those you love and care about, and affirm what you want for them. Try: *I am enjoying our new home in the perfect neighborhood, and my family is elated by this change*; or *I am doing really well in my evening university classes, and my husband and children are enthusiastically supporting me.*

Goooooaaaaalllll!

Remaining Flexible Without Getting Bent Out of Shape

Sometimes we get too caught up in limited ideas about what achieving our goal will look like. What does it mean to be a success or successful in my career? What does it mean to be a good parent? Exploring what it is that you really want will help you find your path, and it will also allow you to be more accepting of the many ways in which your goal might manifest. You can't always know how you'll get to where you want to go.

When I was in my 20s, I had a clear goal that I wanted to be married by age 30. Yet time was ticking away and I still hadn't met Mr. Right. In my late 20s, I was in a relationship with a very nice gentleman who proposed to me . . . and I realized that as important as it was for me to get married, it really wasn't significant that it happen by the time I was 30. What was more important was marrying the right person, and in my heart, I knew this man wasn't the one. Ultimately, I had to be flexible about the timing of my goal.

You might also have to make adjustments with respect to how your goal surfaces. Maybe you'll achieve wealth and abundance in a different form than what you think you need, for example. You may have to reconsider your definitions of success, too. Do you have to be the salesperson with the highest numbers in the office to feel like a success? Do you have to make a certain amount of money? Does being a good parent mean never making a mistake? If you're true to your heart's desire, you'll find that even though the goal you've reached turns out to look very different from what you had expected, you're okay with that and won't become angry or resentful.

The universe has its own ideas about how to make your dreams come true, and you might even be happier with the results it helps you create compared to what you'd initially imagined.

As wonderful as it is to attain the goals you've set for yourself, it's important to recognize that they're not the one thing that will create happiness and fulfillment. I'll always be someone who feels great setting and achieving goals; however, I've also found that the ones that have brought me the most joy are those that are grounded in a passion for helping make the world a better place, even if it's in a small way.

It was nice to be able to afford a good car and a spacious apartment as a result of strong efforts back in my early working days, and I've certainly enjoyed the loving relationships in my life that I've nurtured. But doing the work I do now—helping others achieve their goals and knowing that I can affect people's lives in significant and positive ways—I realize that being productive and successful just isn't enough for me. It seems that for a long time, I'd been overlooking something very important: using my unique set of gifts and talents to contribute to others in meaningful ways. Was giving to others, perhaps, the one thing I'd been seeking?

DO UNTO
OTHERS

*"You will get all you want in life if you
help enough other people get what they want."*

— Zig Ziglar

I've always been ambitious and have had many
goals. But even early on in my sales career, my focus
wasn't on my quota; it was on letting people know about
a product or service they would value. I was genuinely
excited about what I was selling, and my results reflected
that. Back when I sold computer systems and software,
I loved demonstrating my products' features and being
able to show potential clients how our machines could
solve problems they'd been unable to figure out. After I
made the sale—which I often did easily because of my

passion and commitment to matching the product to the customer—I actually enjoyed taking troubleshooting calls to help customers get the most out of the equipment they'd purchased. I recognized that by having these conversations, I was learning more about the product, too—that is, in giving, I was receiving benefits as well. I'd then pass along my newfound knowledge to the next customer, providing even more value.

I loved my job and the money was good, but I began to realize that what made me feel most energized was providing service to others. One day I heard a lecture given by Zig Ziglar in which he said that when you help someone else achieve a goal, you help yourself, and I thought, *Exactly!*

What I learned, however, is that you can't keep score and insist that you get back the same amount you put in. Giving generously without any need to tally how much charity you've provided happens when you've opened your heart, connected to love, and raised the level of each positive emotion that will help you create success and abundance.

Asking, "What can I give that will contribute to others in a beneficial way?" and "How can I serve?" doesn't mean that you'll feel drained or be taken advantage of by others. Instead, it gives you a sense of purpose. Again and again, you can experience making a difference in someone's life in small ways.

The Many Ways in Which We Can Give to Others

Not long ago, I hired a film crew to help me create a commercial for my book *21 Distinctions of Wealth*. We went out on the streets of Ottawa greeting people who'd heard about the shoot from my Website or newsletter. I asked if anyone had a story to share that we could use in our mini-movie, and a lovely young woman named Lisa told me that she'd heard about my work through a friend who had wanted to help her.

Lisa said that she was a young mom who'd been diagnosed with a serious and potentially fatal illness. After doing research on the treatment her physician was recommending, she made a bold decision: she chose to forgo standard medical treatment and work with an alternative-health practitioner. Her doctor and husband were upset, but she was determined. A supportive friend had sent her my books and information about my work in the hopes of helping Lisa learn some ways in which she could manage her thoughts and emotions to maximize healing. She told me that one of my meditations became a key tool she used daily to visualize her body healthy again, and she thanked me for having written books she'd found so helpful. I replied, "You're very welcome—and thank *you* for sharing that with me!"

It had never dawned on me that my advice might actually be used to help someone overcome such a serious health crisis, and I was truly humbled by Lisa's story. To me, just knowing that something I said, wrote, or created was able to affect another person so powerfully was enough to bring tears of joy to my eyes. I told her that I wasn't the one who had done the hard work of listening to that inner voice and using healing techniques every single day to achieve extraordinary results—that was all *her* doing.

I never stop feeling grateful for the opportunity to make a positive contribution to the lives of others—it's

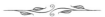
what gives meaning to my own life. I believe that if more people could find their own unique way of serving, they too would experience joy, gratitude, and a strong sense of purpose. When we connect to our deepest passions and talents and bring them forth into the world for the benefit of all, we discover how profoundly we can influence others.

We all have the potential to give in some way; that is, each of us can make our own small corner of the world just a bit brighter and more joyful. Too often we think that if we can't do something big, what's the point? Yet if we give to others from the heart, even a small act can have a very large impact.

Human beings can give in many different ways, but we sometimes overlook the marvelous gifts we have that can be used to assist others. For example, many women are generally taught that they should express sympathy and reach out to people emotionally, while men tend to be taught to help others in more practical ways. Both types of giving are valuable, but sometimes women feel most comfortable offering shoulders to cry on while men prefer to offer constructive support. Then again, others might feel that if they're not donating time, only money, then they're not really offering something of value. What matters most is giving from a place of generosity.

If you start to worry that others will think ill of you if you provided for them in the wrong way, this can be off-putting. By examining the beliefs that have created your discomfort, you can free yourself to give in all sorts of ways and reap the emotional benefits of feeling that you've made a difference in someone else's life.

Next, you'll find three key ways in which you can give to those in need: offering emotional support, sharing our vulnerabilities, and offering practical help.

1. Offering Emotional Support

Although you can't always know what it's like to walk in someone else's shoes, to simply say, "I'm so sorry you're in pain," and offer to help in any way, matters. Take, for instance, a friend of mine who was overwhelmed in dealing with a parent whose health was failing. One day a government bureaucrat who was talking to her about her father's application for social services not only assured her that she would solve the problem that had come up in the process, but also told her, "I'm so sorry that you're going through this. I know it's hard, and I really hope you'll take some time to nurture yourself because caretaking can be so trying. I went through this with my mom and know it can be tough, so you just hang in there and be good to yourself." Now, expressing empathy and compassion was not on this woman's official job description, I'm sure. But she saw the opportunity to give to another, and her words were very comforting to my friend.

Sadly, we sometimes let our own insecurities get in the way of offering emotional support to others. We remain silent out of the fear that we'll say the wrong thing, yet it's never inappropriate to say, "I am so sorry for your loss" or "I wish I could make it better." Simply expressing sympathy is often the best thing we can do for someone who's hurting.

It's important to remember, however, that people's feelings can change. Accept where they are emotionally, but be careful not to imply that certain emotions are right or wrong for them. Years ago I had a girlfriend who was in a bad marriage with a verbally abusive and controlling man. I never liked him, so when she told me she was going to leave him at last because he was so cruel and cold, I agreed with her judgment and told her that she had a right to leave. A few weeks later, she changed her mind . . . and because I'd been so strong in expressing my feelings about her husband, it was uncomfortable between us for a while. That's when I learned that the best thing to do when someone is wrestling with difficult emotions is to say, "This must be so challenging for you," and "I'm always here if you need someone to talk to."

What isn't helpful is to give people even more reasons why they should be feeling bad. Negativity is poisonous, so when you try to comfort others by saying, "Of course you're angry. You have a lot to be upset about!" and go on and on reminding them of all the reasons they have to be furious, you're likely to push them further into anger. So, rather than encourage them to turn up the volume on their negative emotions, simply acknowledge their feelings. Then try to gently guide them into envisioning what their lives would look like if they were feeling happy again.

Those who are in a lot of pain sometimes can't recognize their strengths. It's as if there's a fire and they're in a smoke-filled room, panicked and unable to reach the exit. You can remind them of how they've triumphed over adversity in the past and encourage them to believe in themselves. Tell them about the strengths you've always admired, and inspire them with a story of how someone else overcame a similar challenge. It's also important to offer uplifting words, such as: "I don't know how this is all going to work out, but I'm sure you're going to get through this. You have a right to feel that way—and while I know it's probably hard to believe this right now, in my heart I feel that you're going to end up in a good place. Someday you'll be able look back on this and see how brave you were, as well as the gift that came out of this experience." Simply being reminded that happiness can arise again can give another person hope and faith, which are gifts of tremendous value.

When people I care about are suffering, I encourage them to imagine what good might come out of the situation. The opportunity to wake up to what's really important, achieve a new insight that will serve them in the future, and finally change something that's been a problem for a long time can all be hidden blessings that lie underneath life's challenges. Then I'll try to help my loved ones create a feeling they'd like to experience, perhaps one that's connected to their future. I'll suggest that they envision a time when they're in perfect health again or feeling safe and secure once more. I know that if they can start to acknowledge those positive emotions, they can begin attracting situations that will match up with those feelings.

You can't always talk people out of their dark feelings, but you can plant a seed of positivity that may grow in the future. When the negative sentiment starts to subside just a little, they may remember what you said and be able to embrace it. On the other hand, if you tell them all the ways in which they're justified in being sad, angry, or betrayed, you're adding fuel to the fire. Encourage them to simply accept their feelings in this moment and switch into something more positive. In this way, you'll be sprinkling water on the flames, helping to gently douse them.

You may also feel shy about reaching out to someone you don't know very well because you're uncomfortable with difficult feelings. Believe me, introducing or reintroducing yourself to someone and expressing sympathy can go a long way toward helping this person feel better. It's worth letting go of your insecurity and speaking up.

2. Sharing Our Vulnerabilities

It's easy to feel isolated when life is challenging, as if no one could possibly understand or empathize with what we might be going through. Yet as my friend learned from her experience with the government bureaucrat, just one voice saying "I've been there, too" can provide encouragement and a sense of support.

Focusing on the positive and having faith in the universe is important—yet even people who work hard to remain upbeat and joyful will at times feel scared or insecure. Knowing that others sympathize can lessen those negative feelings; but when many of us see an opportunity to reach out to folks who are in trouble and reassure them that we know what it's like to be in their position, we often hold back. This might be due to the fact that we're afraid they'll resent that we've gotten too personal with them.

For example, I can recall being in my 20s and taking a walk in a park near my home, when I spotted a woman sitting under a tree sobbing quietly. I empathized with her and wondered what I could do to help: *Should I approach her and try to find out what's wrong? Maybe she simply needs to cry and wanted to do it in this beautiful, natural spot. She probably wants to be left alone, and my trying to comfort her would just make things worse.* I felt awkward and ended up silently sending her good wishes and love and continuing on my walk, but I wasn't sure if that had been the best choice.

We can never really know what people want from us unless we ask. We may hesitate because we aren't sure that if we expose our vulnerability, we'll actually help someone . . . but it's always worth the risk to approach our fellow human beings. Sometimes they'll resent the intrusion; if they do, we should recognize that it's only because they're scared, and then show them kindness rather than feel hurt or upset. If we access our compassion, we'll find that we have the strength to withstand their rejection—if someone doesn't accept our outreach gracefully, we're still able to bless them silently on their journey as we move forward on ours.

An example of when I was able to get past feelings of vulnerability to my benefit was the first time I went to a book exposition. I had no predetermined agenda and was simply following the advice of best-selling author Mark Victor Hansen, who'd suggested that I go meet others and learn what I could about marketing the book I'd written and self-published. Instead of allowing myself to feel nervous and appear naïve, I simply carried in my heart the belief that this was a place filled with men and women who would offer me support and advice about getting my book out to as many people as possible. I'd been telling myself that I'd receive many good tips since it was so obvious that my motivation was to put out a positive message that would help others . . . and the expo totally exceeded my expectations! I found that every person I met was gracious, kind, and willing to guide and educate me in whatever way possible—I was totally surprised by the depth of the advice I was offered. Because I approached the situation with an open heart and an intention to connect with others who could help me pursue my dream, I found what I was looking for. I even bumped (literally) into someone who ended up introducing me to countless other helpful people!

On the other hand, I've met individuals who insist that everyone else always has an agenda. They don't believe that they can receive the support they're looking for—perhaps they feel this way because that's just how *they* operate. Nevertheless, I feel compassion for those who have this mind-set, because they're missing out on the joy of giving and receiving freely.

3. Offering Practical Help

When others are suffering, it's only natural to want to help . . . but sometimes it's hard to know what to do. You might feel a sense of lack and think that you have nothing to offer them. However, if you can create positive emotions within yourself, you'll connect to your creativity and find ways to serve.

When people are in crisis, the intensity of their negative emotions increases, which reduces their imagination. This reminds me of a friend of mine who was in such shock and grief after losing her husband that she was overwhelmed by even simple problems at first. While no one could make the pain of his passing go away, those of us who were close to her did what we could to help her figure out a solution to the financial crisis his unexpected death caused and lend her whatever practical help we could.

Several people offered to watch her young children if she needed time alone; others brought prepared meals so that she could have a freezer full of dinners at a time when the last thing she wanted to think about was cooking or eating healthfully. Many months later she told me that one of the kindest things someone had done for her was to go over to her house with his snowblower and clear her driveway and walkway each time it snowed that winter . . . which was something she had always depended on her husband to do. Blowing snow might seem like a small act, but the thoughtfulness displayed by this neighbor truly touched her—he simply saw a need and filled it. Having one less chore to be concerned about helped ease her burden.

Sometimes even offering a piece of key information can help another person. My friend Arielle Ford passed along an idea she'd read about in a book called *The Big Leap*, by Gay Hendricks. This concept is called the "upper-limit problem," and posits that each of us has one problem that we just can't seem to break through. It may be that we're defensive and don't want to develop a new skill or take a risk, we feel undeserving, or we simply may not realize that an upper limit exists. Whatever it is that's blocking us, we're holding ourselves back.

When Arielle, who knows me well, told me about this concept and suggested that I consider exploring it, I immediately recognized that I had my own upper-limit problem: a fear of success. I feared that if I were ultimately successful, work would take up all my time and I wouldn't be able to balance it with everything else in

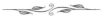
my life. This was interesting for me to think about, but her words made me realize that this limit was there. I wanted to start looking at that ceiling I'd set for myself right away and break through it at last.

It's important to try to see through others' avoidance and point out what they've refused to examine, which can be uncomfortable for everyone involved. If you're offering a strategy and are afraid people might feel defensive and think that you're telling them what to do, there are many ways to give your advice or insight gently. Say, "I don't know if you've ever tried this, but it worked for me," or "I don't know if this will work, but I've heard that other people have dealt with a similar problem successfully by . . ." and offer your strategy. Or say, "I'm not sure if you're even aware of this, but I've noticed something you do that may not be working for you." If you genuinely want to help others find their method of improving a situation, it's easier to find the words that will express your support and give valuable information without seeming like you're trying to tell them what to do. The right piece of information, offered in a loving way, can make a huge difference in someone's life.

When Giving Makes You Uncomfortable

Fears about giving too much and being unfairly used by others can be rooted in past experiences. To open your heart and become generous of spirit again, you have to let yourself be vulnerable and trust that no matter what happens or how others treat you, you'll be okay. In this world, there may indeed be those who will take advantage of you. But when you feel good about yourself and you're giving from a place of joy, abundance, and enthusiasm, you won't attract these people. If they do show up in your life, it's because you're meant to pay attention and learn the lesson of self-love, which requires you to notice when you start to feel used, and then care about yourself enough to say, "This is not okay."

When you start to realize that someone is taking too much from you and not giving back—and then you push aside that uncomfortable sentiment because you don't want to seem foolish, hurt, or angry—you miss the opportunity to learn a lesson. Keep in mind that all emotions are temporary, and the difficult ones exist so that you can make discoveries and grow. Listen to those painful thoughts, and recognize when someone is not treating you well. Don't simply get angry and think, *How dare he!* Create calmness and assure yourself, *Okay, I can see that this is a learning experience.* The calmer you are, the easier it will be for you to see your options, recognize the lesson, and connect to your courage so that you can respectfully confront the other person.

I have a friend named Karen who was trying to help her elderly mother, who could be very angry and demanding. Karen told me, "Sometimes she can be kind and loving, but it's hard for me to relax and just enjoy her good mood—I'm so afraid that if I let myself be vulnerable again, she'll turn around and say something hurtful. I just can't trust her, and that makes me very sad."

The secret to trusting others and remaining open and generous is to understand that *you* are the one who determines your emotions. No one can *make* you feel hurt. You may have a moment in which your automatic response to someone else's behavior is sadness or anger, but you don't have to stoke the fire of that feeling or give

it fuel. Experience it for a few minutes, recognize what you can learn from it, and simply let it go. It will fade away, because all emotions do, no matter how intense they are.

In her head, Karen understood that her mother's behavior wasn't about her; it was the result of the older woman's fear that she was losing control of life. Yet my friend learned that when she would feel an instant emotional response to her mother's behavior, she had to stop for a moment to remind herself what was causing the reaction. Instead of generating thoughts that would increase negative feelings, she'd cut them off and simply remind herself: *Mom's feeling scared and lashing out right now,* creating a sense of compassion for both of them. It also helped to identify what her mother might be feeling and say it out loud: "I know you don't want to go to the doctor's office again, but we have to; besides, it will give us a chance to chat as we're driving. And the leaves on the trees are so beautiful this time of the year—you just have to see them!"

Choosing to be kind turned down the volume on Karen's frustration, and it often had that effect on her mother as well. Switching to positive emotions and words that would soothe her mother allowed Karen to find creative ways to make the situation better. The power of positive emotions gave her the strength to continue to be a giving, generous daughter without wearing herself out.

What Happens When You Give from a Place of Negativity

Sometimes it's possible to give too much and deplete yourself. When this happens, it's almost always because your service to others is rooted in a negative thought, belief, or emotion. If, for example, you feel that someone won't like you or you'll suffer terribly unless you sacrifice to the point of exhaustion, that needs to change. When you begin with generosity and love for *yourself,* as well as for everyone around you, you won't create those sorts of feelings as often. And when you do so, you'll set aside any guilty sentiments and examine why you're holding on to something that's causing you to suffer.

If you're angry and resentful, you can't give lovingly to others. When you sense those destructive feelings arising, you may want to explore them and ask yourself why you had that reaction. Maybe you'll discover an unproductive thought you'd like to discard. If you know the answer, then simply allow yourself to feel that momentarily, noting, *It's okay, this feeling will pass,* and *I don't want to feel this; I'd rather feel something positive.* Then, as the emotion fades, decide on a positive sentiment you'd like to experience instead, and create that feeling in yourself. You might focus on an uplifting thought or create an image in your mind that helps you stay present in a compassionate, confident, or joyful way. Concentrate on your breathing, slowing it down and deepening it, because this will help you switch out of the unfavorable feeling and into a cheerful one. Then you'll have the strength to act in a way that's good for everyone involved. When you love and accept yourself, you'll *always* find ways in which to serve.

Sometimes Karen found that she had to leave the room when her mother became angry and be alone to engage in this process of switching out of a destructive emotion. Her mother would become more agitated, but Karen knew what she had to do in order to return to an attitude of compassion. When she had accomplished that and decided she could go back into the room and face her mother, she would. My friend understood that she couldn't give to anyone else until she replenished her store of positivity. It's just like when you're on an airplane and they tell you that, in the event of an emergency, if you're traveling with a small child you need to put on your own oxygen mask before assisting him or her. You can't give to anyone from a sense of depletion, exhaustion, or frustration.

Even in business, where you're supposed to receive compensation for the work you do, always give to others unconditionally. I can't give a free book or seminar to everyone whose story touches my heart, but at times I *have* donated my products to others and offered them my time and insights without any expectations. I'm very clear on when I want to give my products to someone free of charge because I feel good about myself and know that I'm giving something of value.

It's when people have low self-esteem that they tend to give too much in the hopes of feeling better about themselves. If they don't believe they have anything of value to offer, they may not reach out to anyone, depriving themselves of the joys of giving and receiving. Contributing whatever you can doesn't have to be a painful sacrifice, and you don't have to take a vow of poverty to be a good person. By being honest with yourself about what you need and loving yourself unconditionally, you won't feel desperate for approval or afraid that you won't gain. You'll find the right balance of providing and accepting and will experience the pleasure of making a difference by serving other people with an open heart.

Is serving others the secret to life? I love being able to provide something of value, giving fearlessly, and trusting that the universe will provide. But I've discovered that there's a way to create abundance, joy, and faith within myself that keeps me going even when I'm feeling low and it's hard for me to give: experiencing a sense of gratitude. In fact, thankfulness generates in me such powerful, positive emotions that I've had to wonder: *Is gratitude the one thing?*

Chapter Five

THANK YOU!

*"The correct prayer is never one
of supplication but one of gratitude."*

— NEALE DONALD WALSCH

I have often found great joy in being able to make a difference in other people's lives. However, there was once a time when I realized how difficult it is to continue giving with enthusiasm when not receiving any encouragement, acknowledgment, or thanks in return.

At one point several years ago, I was working for a company I truly believed in. The firm made quality products, and I was willing to go the extra mile to help my customers, so I easily made every sales goal that was set for me. Even so, I gradually began to feel less and less

enthusiastic about my work, and the main reason was my boss. While he was nice enough, he wasn't exactly effusive in his praise: if I made an amazing sale, he'd smile ever so slightly and murmur, "Mmm, very nice, Peggy," and instantly move on to tell me what he expected from me next.

I was very self-motivated, but no matter how well I performed, it seemed that he was about as excited as a dishrag over what I'd accomplished. With so little positive feedback month after month, I began to lose steam. I harbored some thoughts about finding a new job, but by then I was feeling so down that I didn't have much enthusiasm. I meant to update my résumé and make some phone calls, but I just never seemed to get around to it.

Then one day I came across a quote by one of my favorite authors, Melodie Beattie, which said: "Gratitude unlocks the fullness of life. It turns what we have into enough, and more. It turns denial into acceptance, chaos to order, confusion to clarity. It can turn a meal into a feast, a house into a home, a stranger into a friend."

I instantly thought, *That's it! That's what I've been looking for!* I believed that I'd found the formula to feeling like a winner—the secret to success and fulfillment—and decided that I needed to live a life of gratitude. In order to do so, I had to consciously note my many blessings and feel thankful as I thought of each one. Although it would be years before I came across the idea of starting a gratitude journal (which I've now kept up for more than a decade), I began establishing the habit of setting aside time every day to think about all that I was grateful for and feel its power infusing my body.

With gratitude came feelings of hopefulness and confidence, along with curiosity about which direction

my life would take and what bless
my way next. My entire body felt n
that something fantastic was going
I needed was to figure out what I w
know just what to do.

This was a powerful transformat ᴗᴄᴄɪɪ
feeling so low during that time. The sudden and dramatic shift into a profound sense of happiness wasn't even the result of someone building me up with praise—it was me *choosing* to feel positive emotions.

Gratitude for What You Have Today

When you decide to stop resisting your present circumstances, you'll find that you let go of anger, frustration, resentment, sadness, and worry; and this causes you to create positive emotions. You'll be able to see the larger picture of all that's happening instead of zeroing in on the elements you don't like. You'll open yourself up to feeling grateful for everything that's good in your life right now and cherishing all that's positive.

Imagine for a moment that thankfulness is the fuel for a car that can take you anywhere you'd like to go. You can access this powerful vehicle—with its full tank—if you step back and realize its potential. Yet if all you do is notice the car's flaws, saying things like, "There isn't enough legroom . . . this paint color is all wrong . . . this isn't the car I was expecting," you're not going to notice the full tank, the good tires, or the key in your hand that's ready to be inserted into the ignition.

As you let go of any negative feelings about your situation, you start to see what you have to be grateful for.

...may be in good health, but do you state each day, "Thanks for my excellent health! I am so blessed!"? If you do, maybe you won't even notice those little aches and pains.

Focusing on the negative and a sense of lack aren't the results of being unwilling to think positively. Often, when we complain about this or that, we're simply acting out of habit. All day long we're bombarded with advertisements that remind us of everything we don't have. We wouldn't buy so many products and services if we didn't feel a sense of lack and unworthiness—marketers know how to play on those emotions. It takes a conscious effort to shift out of this draining tendency to look at all that's wrong instead of what's right, and then create feelings of appreciation for all that you do have.

The Energy of Gratitude

Gratitude carries with it powerful energy. When you're grateful, you can have fun even when you're working very hard or not seeing immediate results. If you have to force yourself to do what you need to do, the problem may be that you're not feeling this wonderful sense of appreciation. Without it, your tank is empty. You have no fuel to carry you forward.

The way to create a sense of gratitude is to stop and think about all the blessings in your life. The list of what you could feel grateful about is endless: health; relationships with friends, lovers, family members, and neighbors; money and material possessions; intelligence; skills; and so on. Stop yourself in the course of a day, notice your blessings, and proclaim, "I am so lucky!" Be thankful for every little thing. Try walking through your home or down the street one day and coming up with as many things to be appreciative of as you possibly can: *Thank you for this lovely weather. Thank you for my shoes, which are really comfortable. Thank you for my dishwasher, all the food that's in my refrigerator, and the warmth of the sunshine streaming through my window.* Say aloud, "I'm so thankful that I'm healthy and able to make myself a good breakfast this morning. I'm grateful that I have a reliable car to get me to work safely." If you have a short commute, be grateful. If you have a long commute, be grateful—after all, that gives you a block of time to enjoy music, listen to the radio, or recite affirmations.

When you notice the positive aspects of every circumstance in your life, don't just *say* "Lucky me!" *Feel* it! Keep a gratitude journal so that every day you can spend time recording every little thing that contributes to your happiness and sense of good fortune. And notice how energized you are when you make a habit of being—and feeling—grateful.

The more you feel gratitude, the more that feeling can grow. As you do, it will be like a surge of electricity rushing through your house, turning on all the lights and electrical appliances—only in this case, positive feelings and creativity will be turned on. Every positive emotion, from confidence to happiness, will surge in response to your increased gratitude.

It's helpful to think of emotions as being connected and controlled by the same light switch. When you flip the switch on one positive emotion, you automatically turn on every other positive emotion, lifting yourself out of negativity. With all of that energy and light, two things will happen: (1) you'll feel vitalized and eager to

act, and resistance and inertia will drop away; and (2) you'll get in touch with your creativity—the "light" of ideas. Here's a more detailed explanation of these two points:

1. Gratitude Overcomes Obstacles

When you're not feeling appreciative, it can take enormous effort to move forward in life, and the barriers may seem endless. Perceiving so many obstacles will eventually cause you to become fatigued and give up.

Whenever you're facing any form of resistance, gratitude has the power to quickly dissolve it. This is true whether the hindrance comes from inside of you (such as fear or a belief that you can't accomplish your goal, so it's not worth trying) or outside of you (such as a lack of money). Life is much easier when you're grateful—you'll feel powerful, more alive, and enthusiastic—and you'll actually perceive things differently. You see your resources instead of your problems, and when you look again at what's holding you back, those issues won't seem so big after all.

2. Gratitude Opens the Doors to Creativity

When you connect to your inspiration and are able to be resilient—adapting to changes in a positive way—you'll feel the full force of your appreciation. You'll become optimistic and perceive possibilities, and uplifting feelings will surge inside you and open the door to creativity. Once you believe that answers and resources can show up in your life, they will: The universe works to mirror your beliefs. It will prove you right every time.

Ultimately, all mental roadblocks are ones we've fabricated for ourselves. It's creativity that allows us to open up to all the possibilities we haven't yet imagined. The universe isn't trying to make our lives difficult; it's only reflecting back to us what we've created. When we change what's within, what's outside of us changes in response.

When your mind is focused on the good in your life—all the tools, people, information, money, emotional support, and resources you have available—you'll find yourself able to accept that nothing remains the same, and you'll remember that you can always choose your emotions. So if you want to change your circumstances, you have the power to do so. Start on the inside: put the key in the ignition and let the fuel of gratitude propel you down the road toward something better. You'll almost instantly feel empowered, excited, optimistic, and curious about what lies ahead. Because you'll be moving forward enthusiastically, you'll start seeing opportunities appear, avenues that will take you toward your goal without your having to struggle so hard to make things work or figure out what to do. Superhighways will suddenly show up in front of you so that you can get off the rutted and winding back roads, speed up, set the cruise control, and know you're on your desired destination.

Many people feel that they aren't creative enough, but I'm not talking about being a songwriter or painter. I'm referring to being in touch with your ability to approach life with wonder, curiosity, and enthusiasm. Creativity lets you become resilient—you learn to trust that there can be an innovative breakthrough or amazing new opportunity just around the corner.

This resourcefulness also gives you the courage to take risks because you know that if something doesn't work out, there will be other chances: you'll actually be able to see how you can switch gears and try something new. Priming the pump of your creativity will make it easier for you to handle unexpected changes or bumps in the road. You'll feel certain that there's a way to get past life's challenges and create a better situation.

When you allow yourself to get in touch with your creativity, you'll find that you can access it quickly. (I know that I don't have to be alone in the woods for three weeks to get into a creative mode—I can get a great idea in the 15 minutes while I'm driving my son, Michel, to school or while I'm in the shower.) Even if you have no talent for the arts, sketching, painting, dancing, or writing poetry are all terrific ways to get in touch with your vision of originality. Or just try meditating; people who practice this regularly say that it allows them to be more creative.

Remember, all positive emotions enhance each other, so if you're feeling wonder and excitement, you'll feel gratitude as well. Instead of resenting challenges and changes, you'll feel grateful for the opportunities they present.

Being at Peace with What Is

Instead of thinking about what could have been or what might be, focus on all that is good in your life and create a feeling of gratitude. If you do, you'll find peace.

Thank You!

Recently, when my mother was very sick, I was spending a lot of time at her side, lending her emotional support and communicating with her doctors and caretakers, along with my family members, to make sure that her needs were being met. At times I'd feel a little anxious about taking so much time off from work. (I'm not used to being away from my computer and phone for long . . . my husband, Denis, likes to tease me and say that my idea of a vacation is *only* getting in four hours of work a day.) But as my family members and I rotated around-the-clock shifts at the hospital, I found myself accepting the rhythm of my life at this very special time.

I realized that despite all that was going on, I was having my best year in business yet. I was having to turn down work, in fact. Why shouldn't I trust that more opportunities would come to me? Worrying was making me feel unproductive and drained, so whenever I found myself distressed, I'd switch into creating a feeling of gratitude. I had to remind myself that I was thankful for all the opportunities and clients I had and for having the flexibility and financial security to be able to spend this time with my mother.

My gratitude made it easier to remain fully present with my clients when I was working; in addition, I regularly took the time to be thankful for the opportunity to continue serving others, helping them achieve their dreams. Gratitude gave me the strength to do all that I had to do, despite having so many demands on my time. Things somehow got done without my having to struggle to make them happen. I had plugged into the power of positive emotions and felt confident that at any given time I was making the right choice for everyone. I was at my computer when I needed to get work done and at my mother's bedside when I needed to be there for her. I was very sad, but I also felt a deep sense of acceptance and grace. In my heart, I knew that everything was exactly as it was meant to be.

Letting Go of Striving

It's good to have passions and goals and to be productive and successful, but letting success define you can result in your feeling bad about yourself if you should hit an obstacle or not achieve all that you set out to do. It's possible to be at peace with what is without constantly striving for improvement. Gratitude gives you the ability to go with the flow and accept that life has its challenges, and that sometimes it will seem that you're stuck. It allows you to open up to new ideas and trust that they will show up in due time.

Most of us can't bear to remain for very long stretches in a state of stagnation, waiting for circumstances to shift. But it's easy to become caught up in our expectations of how life *should* be. We scramble to fix problems, measuring ourselves by our achievements and how much we've accomplished in a certain period of time. I'm reminded of something a friend of mine told me years ago: "I need to make a salary that starts with a three by the time I'm 30." This was an interesting goal, but when she didn't quite meet it, she became very upset. While she was in a job full of opportunities, not having hit that particular mark blinded her to all that she could be appreciating about her life.

Please note that there's a difference between acceptance and passivity. Acceptance is the choice to be at peace with what's happening right now, even as you're creating the positive feelings that will allow you to bring about something great in the future. It's always accompanied by the force of positive emotions. Passivity, on the other hand, is characterized by not experiencing any strong emotions. In other words, you're being passive when you go through your days robotically, doing just what needs to be done at work and no more, eating a dinner you don't enjoy and savor, and turning on the boob tube to kill time before bed. It's not that you have to dress up and go dancing every night, but if you aren't feeling any strong, positive emotions, you'll be uncreative and uninspired. You won't make yourself do something different, whether it's trying to cook a new meal, starting an interesting conversation over dinner, or spending the evening attempting an activity you've always said you wanted to do but never seemed to make time for.

Passivity involves distraction, lethargy, and avoidance. If you're passive, you'll start to see your mood slipping into melancholy and then sadness . . . or even depression. The key to avoiding this is to create a feeling of gratitude for the simple pleasures, as well as the abundance, in your life.

To enhance my feelings of gratitude, every day for years I've worked with affirmations and something I call a Power Life Script: a 20-minute-long recording I've made of myself reciting what I value most in my life (whether or not I actually have all that I long for right now in the present moment), affirming all that I'm grateful for. I'm not driven to do it out of a sense fear that something bad will happen if I don't, nor am I driven by the idea that I must do this if I'm to reach my goals—it's simply

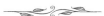

a habit. The actual process of creating the life I want for myself by envisioning how I'd like it to be, focusing on the emotions I'll feel when I achieve my goals, and having faith that the universe will bring to me all that I need are such enriching and energizing actions that I perform these rituals even when it's inconvenient to do so.

Of course everyone has off days or unexpected interruptions, but I've developed the self-discipline to express gratitude daily by using these techniques because the feelings themselves are so wonderful.

We can all find the discipline and impetus to follow through on our commitments when we experience the incredible power and happiness that's generated when we concentrate on what we value.

Gratitude When the Work Is Hard

It's a myth that if it's work, it can't be fun. Even if a task is very challenging, you can feel grateful while doing it. If you let yourself feel unproductive or negative emotions, such as worry or resentment, the work will seem harder and take longer.

Occasionally, the authors I work with are reluctant to commit to the type and amount of work they have to be willing to do in order to make their book a success. They'll ask me about ways to avoid making a lot of phone calls or doing a lot of research—or they'll say, "This sounds a lot like a sales job," as if that were a bad thing. My response is, "If you really believe in what you're doing, what would happen if you let your excitement course through you as you make those sales calls? How about feeling grateful about the opportunity to help

others by letting them know what you can offer them?"
Years ago, I realized that cold-calling can seem intimidating and awful because of the name it was given. Who wants to call someone "coldly," without giving or receiving any warmth? I prefer to think of phoning someone I've never met as "relationship building." Whenever I cold-call, I send out warmth, feeling grateful for the opportunity to improve people's lives in some small way . . . and then, more often than not, they're kind and gracious to me even if they're not interested in what I'm offering.

When you're feeling unenthusiastic about the hard work you're having to do, remind yourself of *why* you're doing it. If the work isn't coming naturally, maybe you don't believe in what you're doing, selling, or saying. Think about what you really want to do, and do it. You may be very surprised by how grateful you are for the chance to do what you love.

A client of mine generated a very extensive e-mail campaign for her book using a letter that began: "I am the parent of a special-needs child." Every time she saw that opening line in the e-mail she'd composed, she felt a connection to the person she was e-mailing—whether this individual was an educator, physician, therapist, or director of a day-care center or preschool. She imagined their compassion for other special-needs children, felt thankfulness for all the people who help them, and then hit SEND. I wasn't surprised to hear that her gratitude generated more of the same. She received many e-mail responses thanking her for the notification about her book, praising her for the work she was doing, and wishing her the very best. It's no wonder she had the patience to continue sending e-mails, sometimes for hours a day.

Each time she sent one or got a response, she connected with a feeling of gratitude and happiness. As she told me, "Whenever I send an e-mail, I think about how someone will buy my book, learn something about helping these kids, and actually be able to make a child's life better. Getting the word out is addictive! I am *so* grateful that I can reach these people and let them know about this resource."

Growing Your Appreciation

If you appreciate your spouse and children, you grow your gratitude ("appreciation" means an increase in value or amount). When you become more thankful, this makes you feel and act more lovingly. Remember when you first fell in love? It probably seemed as if you were walking on air because you were so happy. You felt so much joy and compassion that it spilled over into every area of your life. When you're that happy, you even look different! Every cell in your body vibrates at a higher level, making you healthier and more energetic.

Every day, I appreciate Denis, who is my soul mate. I tell him how much I love and appreciate him. When I write in my gratitude journal each night, I express how thankful I am to have him in my life. Denis likes to say, "Happy wife, happy life," because he knows that my happiness enhances his happiness. We lift each other up, raising the level of joy in our home.

Some people have been brought up to believe that it's not all that important to express gratitude, but they don't realize its power. Or they're shy about thanking others, thinking it's "mushy" or that it makes them

look weak or foolish. Never underestimate the value of gratitude and its ability to lift you up. Create a sense of confidence and it will be easier to show that you're truly thankful. You'll find the right words because they'll come from the heart.

Appreciate even those circumstances or relationships that you tend to think of as negative by finding the value in them. If you're experiencing regret, thinking, *I really shouldn't have done it that way,* try this instead: *I'm grateful to realize there's a better way to handle it, and I'm going to respond with love.* Be glad you have a chance to grow, learn, and make your life better. You can't always control your circumstances, but you can always choose your attitude. If you have difficulty feeling grateful, feel curious. Muse on what valuable lesson is available to you right now as a result of the challenges you're facing. Ask yourself, "How can this situation serve me or others, teach me something, make me laugh, or strengthen me?" The more grateful you are, the more positive you'll be. Your life will seem perfect just as it is.

In fact, for a long time I believed that perfection *was* the ultimate goal—that by serving others unconditionally; achieving my goals; and feeling wonderful, positive emotions such as gratitude, I could fix all my problems and live a perfect life. After all, why not aim for the very top—a life completely free of troubles and sadness? *Maybe,* I thought, *the one thing is perfection itself.*

Chapter Six

CROSS ALL YOUR *T*'S AND DOT ALL YOUR *I*'S

"Never neglect the little things. Never skimp on that extra effort, that additional few minutes, that soft word of praise or thanks, that delivery of the very best that you can do. It does not matter what others think, it is of prime importance, however, what you think about you. You can never do your best, which should always be your trademark, if you are cutting corners and shirking responsibilities. You are special. Act it. Never neglect the little things!"

— OG MANDINO

When I first saw a motivational speaker make a presentation at a meeting held by my company, I realized that I had the ability to change my life, and I developed an eagerness to learn more about self-empowerment.

85

Over the years, I've been inspired by many lectures given by teachers, workshop leaders, and authors—some of whom had reassuring, low-key presenting styles, while others gave energetic and entertaining talks. Whenever I saw them address audiences, the programs seemed polished, and I was totally impressed by the presenters' mastery of the material and their ease in speaking to large groups. If an audience member asked a question, the speakers answered easily and without stumbling, because they were fully present in what they were doing and their minds were sharp. They were also good listeners and paid close attention to how people were receiving the information, and I greatly admired the dedication to their work that they exhibited.

Looking at my mentors and how positive they were, I decided that I too wanted to help others reach their goals. *To do this,* I thought, *I'll have to be the poster girl for success.*

Now, of course, I had to convince others of the value of my advice and prove my integrity. If I couldn't "walk the walk," my message would have no value. But I felt that being successful wasn't enough to prove my credibility—my accomplishments had to be unquestionable. The more I thought about the importance of attending to all these details, the more I became convinced that being a flawless role model for others would ultimately be what would lead me to happiness and fulfillment.

It's All in the Details

People who don't meet their goals often haven't realized just how important it is to focus on the details.

It's said that movie star Bette Davis once stopped filming a scene in one of her movies to point out to the director that a klieg light—one of hundreds—had burned out and needed to be changed before they proceeded. Miss Davis was so aware of every aspect of her work that she noticed this minute detail. Her attention to the little things that affected how she appeared on-screen helped ensure her long career in Hollywood. Her understanding of how lighting impacted her appearance allowed her to look her very best despite any signs of aging (this being in an era when actresses had to possess absolutely flawless beauty to be cast in leading roles).

I am a strong believer in concentrating on the particulars in the areas of life that matter to you most. For example, there's nothing more reassuring than hiring someone who always looks completely pulled together and perfectly accessorized to help you choose a wardrobe. This describes my friend Diane Craig, who's a highly successful image consultant, to a tee. Or think about the peace of mind you'd have with the accountant who finds every last deduction you could take and each figure that doesn't look right, or the teacher who can tell you that your child is struggling with handwriting and it's affecting his ability to complete his homework. Aren't these the professionals you want in your life?

Being aware of the details and getting them right shows a dedication and integrity that's very admirable. I wanted to be that way and have my clients know that they could always count on me. I took great pride in knowing that by being detail oriented, I was providing excellent service and value.

The Pressure of Perfectionism

Although I've almost always felt confident about my drive, ambition, and eagle eye for detail, the truth is that I used to worry too much about getting every little thing right in every situation. Deep down, I was afraid of what people would think if I wasn't absolutely impeccable in all areas of my life, and the pressure I put on myself was tremendous. If I made even the smallest mistake, or something I created didn't turn out exactly as I'd expected, I'd become upset and criticize myself very harshly. Negative emotions would arise, and old feelings of low self-worth would surface.

Knowing how bad I felt whenever I didn't meet my extremely high standards, I did everything possible to ensure that I didn't make a single mistake or disappoint anyone. For instance, although I felt that my first book was well written and contained valuable information, that wasn't enough for me. I believed that I needed to have it printed on the highest-quality paper, using the very best materials, and with the edges gold embossed. I hired a company—recommended by a friend—that promised they would procure only the best editor, typesetter, and book designer to work on the project. Had I been less afraid of making a mistake, I would have trusted myself to find these professionals on my own and saved a lot of money. Instead, I believed that I had to rely on others who seemed to know more than I did.

And then, when I finally held the completed book in my hand, I was shocked to discover that it contained five typographical or spelling errors . . . *after all I'd put into it!* I temporarily lost sight of the value the book provided—the other 53,995 words that were spelled and printed

correctly—and felt awful, even believing that people would judge me negatively because my book contained a few typos.

Eventually, I knew that I'd have to change my emotions if I was going to promote the book enthusiastically. As I calmed down, I realized that the situation wasn't a total disaster, which was how it had felt at first. Looking back now, I can see that I was too demanding because of my insecurities and unforgiving perfectionism. If *this* book happens to have an error or two in it, I'll know that I didn't disappoint anyone and that there's no need to feel bad about myself.

We should all do our very best at what matters to us, but then, if our accomplishments aren't utterly perfect, we need to accept that without becoming angry, sad, or frustrated. Personally, I've come to learn that, when taken to extremes, the pursuit of flawlessness leads to feeling bad, losing track of priorities, and even being burned out by the pressure of having to live up to the unrealistic standard of excellence at all times.

Perfectionism—an unwillingness to accept *any* mistakes whatsoever—often stems from anxiousness. You may think that you have to get every single detail right and end up missing the forest for the trees, losing sight of what you value most. The reality is that you can't be perfect at all times; you must choose those things in your life that you're willing to let go of, because you'll become overwhelmed if you don't.

This brings to mind the appearance of my yard at home. Many of my neighbors have meticulous landscaping with creative displays of bushes and flowers—my house, on the other hand, has the landscaping it had when I bought it. I just don't care enough to do more than minimal upkeep, so I don't try to make my yard fancier. If the sprinklers don't work just right, or I return from vacation and a few of the plants look wilted, my attitude is, "Oh well, we'll try to bring them back to life."

I also don't care if I ever learn how to use all the functions on my cell phone and computer or master every piece of technology that I own. If I have a few minutes to spare, I'm not going to browse my phone's menus looking for applications I didn't know about; I'm going to spend it doing something I love. I've come to realize that if I try to be perfect in every area of my life, I'll never be able to do it all, and I'll just end up exhausted.

By releasing any feelings of anxiousness or insecurity, I'm able to connect to my positive feelings and be energized and enthusiastic. With those powerful emotions fueling me, I'm able to do more and attend to the details that *do* matter to me.

When Others Expect You to Be Perfect

Sometimes, even if you do your best and have a healthy amount of concern for getting the details right, others will insist on your being perfect because of their own fears or insecurities. Not long ago, a friend shared a blog with me that had some interesting ideas about healthy eating. I decided to check out the readers' comments for even more good suggestions, since I enjoy cooking. Yet as I scrolled through some of the postings, I saw that several people were horrified that the blog—which is associated with a major newspaper—included the word *veggies* instead of *vegetables*. While the blogger

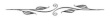

probably should have considered using the more formal word, I quickly stopped reading because comment after comment railed at her with anger because she'd used the "wrong" word and "ruined" the blog. Such perfectionism blinds us to the substance of things and generates anger, worry, and defensiveness. I was happy to see that the blogger, while apologetic, seemed as baffled by the outcry as I was, yet seemed to have a sense of humor about it. Some people would have felt so attacked in that situation that they would have given up and stopped writing altogether, but it was nice to see that this woman was able to deal with the criticism so gracefully.

Others will often give up on projects and dreams because they're afraid of being hurt by criticism if they make a mistake. I know that in my perfectionist days, not only was I hard on myself, but I was a people pleaser, too. I took it completely to heart if just one person criticized me—a negative response like the one the blogger received would have been devastating to me.

If your parents overlooked the *A*'s on your report card and only wanted to talk to you about the sole *B*, or if they insisted that you not leave the house if a hair was out of place, you may have internalized their standards of perfection and believed that they felt you weren't good enough. They may not have realized that they were sending you this message with their behavior, but if you developed low self-worth, this could have been a contributing factor. You may have grown up to be just as hard on yourself as your parents were on you—or you just gave up on the idea of achieving your goals, thinking that you couldn't possibly succeed.

The fact is that we're all perfect just as we are, even if we're sometimes irritable or make mistakes. After I spent

more time around motivational speakers and the people who worked with them, I discovered that my heroes— those I considered to be icons of success—all had their off days. I heard stories of presenters who were known for momentarily losing their temper and authors who wrote eloquently about the importance of compassion and harmony yet acted competitive among their peers. One person in particular was so insecure and anxious about her appearance that she would sometimes be more concerned with how she looked than how she was treating other people. I had to admit that, just like me, many of these people had their flaws and couldn't always live up to their own ideals.

At first I felt disappointed to discover that my heroes weren't perfect, but then I became somewhat relieved to understand that they're only human after all. I still had just as much respect and admiration for them, but I also realized that I didn't have to put so much pressure on myself to never make a mistake or have a bad day. I began to recognize that they truly believed in what they were saying and did their best to live by it. What made them professionals was that even on the days when they were feeling a little blue or worrying about how others might perceive them, they did their very best to be an inspiration. It's not that they were hypocritical; they were simply striving like everyone else to meet their high standards and struggling when they didn't always meet the mark they set for themselves.

Moving Toward a Healthier Solution

There's a danger in believing that we can have total mastery over not just outcomes, but our feelings and thoughts as well. We can become obsessed about control if we start thinking that we're failures if we let our negative emotions surface even for a moment. We have the capacity to be angry, sad, jealous, or doubtful for a reason—there's a purpose to every challenge. As Neale Donald Walsch wrote in his book *Friendship with God:* ". . . God's perfect beings may do imperfect things—or what we would *call* imperfect things—yet everything that occurs in life occurs for a perfect reason. There is no such thing as a mistake in God's world, and nothing happens by chance."

To me, perfection means that you're feeling content and grateful, connected to your vital, positive energy—that you're able to *be* in the moment. For example, you might be grieving over a terrible loss and realize that perfection is in the beauty of your love for the person who has passed away. If you've just heard a news report about a tragedy and you feel compassionate for the person who was hurt . . . well, what could be more perfect than the way your heart works? Sometimes your emotions rise up so suddenly and unexpectedly that you're left deeply humbled.

When you're finally able to let go of perfectionism, you can face your failings and see the positive aspects you're able to take from them. To that end, when I published my first book—spending more money than I needed to in order to reach my goal—I can now say that I could have made a better choice. But I also think that I created an opportunity for myself to learn something

valuable: to trust in myself (and my ability to find top-notch professionals) and the importance of getting more than one opinion before making a decision. In addition, I learned to focus on my priorities and release any need for every detail to be perfect. Eventually, I was able to be proud of my book, grateful to all those who'd helped me, and enthusiastic about promoting it because I appreciated its value despite those five typos.

Today, my priorities are very clear to me. One of them is that I want to spend time with my husband and son and not travel too much. When someone recently offered me an excellent business opportunity that would have meant more time away from home, I didn't feel the need to show anyone what a perfect success story I was by seizing the chance to make more money. I recognized that if I remained true to my deepest values, I'd have all I needed: money, opportunities, and joy.

There are times when someone will ask me to do something at the last minute, and I'll say no without feeling guilty. It's not because I don't want to help out; I've just learned to cut myself some slack and stop being such a people pleaser.

I still care about the important details, because I do believe they matter. For instance, an author I've worked with in the past told me that she just hired someone to set up a Website for the Internet-marketing campaign she was launching, and I decided to check it out the other night to make sure it was working properly. It wasn't my responsibility to do so—that wasn't part of my agreement with her—but I knew it was important to her for it to be functioning at 100 percent, so I checked it and let her know about a glitch I'd found.

When you're in business for yourself and doing something you love, and yours is a personality that tends

toward perfectionism, it can be difficult to set boundaries with clients because you're so eager to help them.

My point is illustrated by the story of a consultant I know. He told me that he'd wanted to please his customers so much that he hadn't been allowing himself enough time to complete tasks for them. If they asked him to do something, he'd immediately promise to do it and get back to them by the end of the day. Then he'd feel stressed out and angry about the pressure he'd placed on himself . . . and he'd even get upset with his clients! It finally occurred to him that even if he could complete a task by that afternoon, he didn't always have to *promise* that it would be done by then. He could buy himself an extra day or so when he knew the customer would be okay with waiting a little longer.

By saying, "Sure, I can do that and get it to you by the end of the week," he let go of his anxious perfectionism and was able to attend to all the tasks and details with calmness, enthusiasm, and confidence, knowing that he'd still meet his goals. He even found that by alleviating so much stress, he was energized enough to get his work done quickly, and he stopped getting angry at himself or resenting his customers (after all, he realized that *he* was the one who was creating the pressure he was feeling!).

Life Doesn't Always Demand Perfection

Life is a work in progress. If you have to have everything "just so" before you allow yourself to feel content and happy, you miss out on the perfection that already exists and the opportunities to create joy and gratitude

right now, in this moment. When you attend a holiday gathering, you don't have to wear the most splendid outfit or bring the perfect side dish. If you aim for that, you may become so hung up on getting every detail just right that you arrive late and hold up dinner! This is a metaphor for life: let go of any feelings of inadequacy or unworthiness, be clear about your priorities, and show up having done the very best you can . . . and then don't obsess over the results.

Not everyone will share your passions or be as enthusiastic about your goals as you are. When you work with others, recognize that they may have very different priorities. I learned this lesson years ago when corporations would hire me to talk to their employees. I'd go to boardrooms, set up for my presentations, and be all fired up to teach these employees how to work better as teams or set individual goals that aligned with the company's. The men and women would file in and take their seats, and I'd look around the room and see that some of them had the "Who are you and why should I listen to what you have to say?" attitude. While some were eager to learn, others had no interest in bettering themselves, and it can be very challenging to work with people who are uninspired and miserable. Keeping the energy in the room high was difficult when certain individuals were expressing so much negativity.

If you genuinely wish to bring value to the world, it will be easier for you to deal with people who resist your positive efforts to help them. You'll assist them as much as you can, but you'll also realize when it's time to move on and help those who are willing to receive what you're offering.

If you're solely focused on perfection, you'll feel that nothing is good enough, and it will make you exhausted. No matter how hard you work, too much emphasis on examining every minute detail of your problems will hold you back from overcoming them. Paying attention to what truly matters, however, generates satisfaction, joy, and contentment about a current situation even as you're moving toward your goals. This wonderful balance of feeling good about a situation as it is and enthused about making it better is wonderfully energizing.

Attending to details in a conscious way allows you to recognize that mistakes are learning experiences, and it gives you the courage to admit when you don't like the results you've achieved. You may suffer through sadness or frustration once you've decided that something isn't working for you, but then you'll be able to let those emotions go and focus on creating positive feelings. When you do so, you can move forward instead of getting stuck in regret.

Sometimes people will feel so intimidated thinking that others are disappointed in them that they hang on to guilt and shame for a very long time, regardless of evidence that the person who they believe they've let down has moved on. For example, I had a client who was almost obsessed with fixing a problem in her past, but when she finally confronted the person she'd wronged, he was dumbfounded. He'd actually forgotten the entire incident, while she was the only one holding on to it and judging herself negatively because of a mistake she thought she'd made.

Harsh Critics and Admitting to Mistakes

Because we all make mistakes and have room for improvement, we'll sometimes be judged. People don't necessarily know how to give gentle, constructive criticism; and if we're sensitive to it (as I am), we may dread hearing it.

I prefer not to receive unsolicited feedback from others, but I still ask for advice at times. I know that if I simply reflect on how I might further my career or personal life, I'll come up with many ways in which I can improve. Knowing that there's always the possibility of doing better, I set aside plenty of time for self-examination.

I can be a very harsh self-critic, but I've finally learned that this reflection process can be a constructive one. If I start to feel bad about myself as I reflect on how I handled a particular client or delivered a speech, I stop, breathe, and switch into a more positive mind-set. Regardless of which emotions I choose to create, my confidence will rise and allow me to be honest about my mistakes and see where I might avoid them next time. Before, when I was a perfectionist, I could work myself into a state of frustration over the smallest flaw, which did nothing to help me in any way. Uplifting results always stem from positive—not negative—feelings.

We can be extremely harsh judges of ourselves and make unfair comparisons to others—noting how wonderfully the person next door handles her kids or how brilliantly co-workers deal with deadlines—not recognizing that they have their own challenges as well. We may not be aware of others' troubles or think that their issues are such a big deal, but no one knows what it's like to be in another's situation.

For instance, I have a friend who struggles to try to improve her eating habits, feeling terrible about herself when she doesn't live up to her high standards. Yet this issue isn't evident by looking at her because she isn't overweight, has beautiful skin, and appears to be in excellent health. Now, my friend would never criticize the way anyone else chooses to eat, but she's convinced that her own habits are the absolute worst. This woman's self-image seems completely out of sync with what others see—by letting go of her perfectionism, she could develop a less distorted image of herself and discover and embrace her beauty.

When I finally said good-bye to my own anxiety-driven perfectionism, I experienced a sense of contentment and joy that I'd been missing. I'd always believed that if I worked very hard, doing everything possible to reach the pinnacle of success, I'd achieve my goals and be happy . . . but then it started occurring to me that maybe it was the other way around. I realized that by letting go of perfectionism and anxiety, I'd feel comfortable with what I was doing and increase my sense of joy; and that seemed to go hand in hand with more opportunities and success. *Maybe*, I thought, *happiness isn't a destination point, but the path itself: the route that leads to everything good in life. Maybe the one thing is to simply be happy.*

Chapter Seven

HAPPILY EVER AFTER

"There is no way to happiness. Happiness is the way."

— Dr. Wayne W. Dyer

For many years I tried to put my finger on that key to success and fulfillment . . . which would also put an end to my sense of restlessness.

I went to seminars and workshops, listened to scores of inspirational audiotapes, meditated, fire-walked half a dozen times, and bought virtually every self-help book I could find. I thought that maybe Bob Proctor, Anthony Robbins, Denis Waitley, Og Mandino, or some other motivational speaker might have the answer. And while I did learn and grow a lot as a result of hearing their insights, I still felt that something was missing.

Then I heard Wayne Dyer say, "There is no way to happiness. Happiness is the way," and I immediately thought, *If happiness isn't a destination but the journey itself, it has to be the answer to all my problems, right?* With that, I decided to learn all that I could about the subject.

Happiness Is Simple

When I think of happiness, I can't help but think of children, who express joy so easily and without hesitation. I can remember when my son and his friends were around five or six years old, and they just loved it when I'd take them with me to the car wash. It was so much fun for them to sit in the car and watch those brushes and the soapy water sweep over the car, and they'd chatter away and squeal in delight.

Unfortunately, we older folks forget just how easy it is to create happiness. Too often we put limitations on our high spirits instead of just enjoying the simple pleasures of life, or we find all sorts of ways to talk ourselves out of feeling lighthearted. It's great to focus on a set of goals, but to have a list of conditions for what will make us feel good complicates life and makes it difficult to simply experience contentment.

Instead of feeling joyful and exuberant, we start to worry and feel restless as we think, *Yes, okay, I suppose I could be happy about the good things in my life right now, but I have so many problems to think about.* We falsely believe that happiness can't be experienced until we get rid of all of those problems—it turns out that the absence of challenges from our lives doesn't automatically bring us satisfaction. We can create pleasure whenever we choose, and it isn't an end point that's reached by clearing away all the obstacles on the road leading to it—the barriers are all in our heads.

To be happy, we must learn to tame our minds so that they don't continually generate thoughts that lead to negative emotions, and it takes practice to bring about delight in all that we do.

In fact, there's a new branch of psychology called positive psychology that focuses on helping folks create happiness and positive emotions rather than fixing problems. So many people have internalized the false belief that life requires suffering—that no matter how well their lives are going, all they can think about is what's wrong and how to fix it. They don't recognize the value in acknowledging their problems and working on them while remaining happy, regardless of how bad things seem to be. They'd actually find that their experiences would be completely different if they only focused on creating more of what makes them feel good.

We're especially likely to focus on concerns that we have in long-term relationships because over time, we just naturally notice our partner's flaws (or, as I prefer to call them, "quirks"). Yet in order to create happiness, we must look at our relationships and ask, "What can I appreciate in this person and feel grateful for?" If we decide to focus on those little things that annoy us about them, our excitement to be with them will fizzle out.

Of course, we all have priorities and breaking points in our relationships, but when life is going pretty well, it's very easy to start zeroing in on those idiosyncrasies that bother us and use them as excuses to create unrest. To that end, whenever I read Dear Abby, I'm usually amused by the sorts of problems people feel compelled to write to her about—they'll express irritation about how their partner always leaves dirty laundry on the floor or coffee rings on the counter. Very often, Abby will wisely point out that while there may be solutions to these little problems, the individuals writing in shouldn't cloud their perceptions so that they're constantly focused on the negative. Everyone has pet peeves, but when these complaints lower the level of happiness, it's time to let go of the small stuff.

In Praise of Happiness

Happiness is like a major ingredient in a recipe, in that there's no substitute for it. It would be like making a batch of cookies and forgetting to put in the sugar: they just wouldn't taste right.

Many people in the Victorian era believed that the purpose of life was to be a good person and would have rejected the idea that happiness is important, viewing the desire for it as selfish. I believe something very different: the way to being an honorable person is to feel happy.

When you're full of joy, you want to help others experience it, too. When you *feel* good, you're inspired to *do* good. Your own bliss naturally flows outward from you and benefits others, just as you receive the positive emotions of others. Happiness connects you to others as you lift them up through sharing your joy—it's infectious. You can be in an awful mood, yet if a stranger cracks a funny joke, you quickly find yourself laughing, lightening up, and feeling better.

Optimism increases your own sense of well-being, so it's completely unselfish to take care of yourself. If you try to *be* good without *feeling* it, you'll often end up giving to others from a place of negativity, which leads to more melancholy. You may be able to help people, but you'll probably do so grudgingly—you'll feel that you don't have enough to offer, and you'll think that by giving, you'll be depleting yourself. You may also resent that others aren't reciprocating and filling the void of unhappiness within you (as if they could!). Immerse yourself in powerful, positive emotions before trying to do good in the world and you'll be like a cup overflowing with boundless energy, giving generously and fearlessly.

Happiness is connected to all other positive emotions, so when you feel it, you'll become more confident, curious, calm, and loving as well. At first you might resist it because you feel embarrassed and don't recognize the value of joy—as if being happy were a sign of simplemindedness or foolishness. Or you'll feel guilty for being so cheerful if others aren't feeling the same way. The reality is that no one benefits from your displeasure; if you want to help those who are suffering, *don't* join them in their sadness. Empathize, but generate happiness and help them discover their own capacity for it. You can do this by expressing love instead of telling them not to feel bad. Whenever people are troubled and someone reaches out to help with compassion, it's easier for them to return to a state of happiness.

When I figured out that my cheerful nature benefits others as well as me, I started to allow myself to act this way more often, making a conscious choice to create joy every day. Whenever I felt upset, I'd remind myself that joy is a far better, more powerful emotion, and I switched into feeling it. Then I would savor that feeling by appreciating and growing it.

Savoring happiness is a vital part of this process. I know that this can be challenging, though, because life seems to rush by so quickly that we start to think we have to move on to the next thing right away or we'll get left behind.

This reminds me of an editor I know, who told me what she used to do when she worked in a publishing house years ago and someone would bring her the first copy of a book she'd been working on for many months: she'd look it over, admire it for a few seconds, and then put it down and immediately get back to work. No wonder this woman became burned out at her job!

If you only allow yourself to experience joy briefly before turning your attention to the next task, it's going to be very hard to keep your morale high. Celebrate what's good in your life; and focus on your pleasures, not your problems.

Gratitude and happiness are intertwined, because when you feel thankful for what you have, you can't help but be cheerful. You can also create happiness simply by letting images that bring you joy enter your mind; in addition, you can change your mind-set by looking around and noticing what's positive, beautiful, and wonderful in your life. Take a moment right now to observe your surroundings and find something that's beautiful or wondrous. Just sit there, look around, and allow bliss to rise within you.

Conditional Happiness

If you're rigid in your notions about what will make you happy, it's probably because you're feeling anxious and fearful, wanting to control your circumstances, the people around you, and your future. However, the way to deal with those hidden emotions is not to set strict conditions for what you need in order to be happy, but to *heal* those emotions by replacing them with joy.

We all have different likes and dislikes and hopes and dreams. Some of us like to live in a rural area with lots of space and solitude, and others thrive in a noisy, bustling city. And there are those who like an orderly environment, while many prefer to live in a bit of a mess. We might not even realize what our priorities or preferences are until we've experienced something new . . . and then we suddenly recognize that we've taken certain circumstances for granted. When things change and we don't like them, we might think: *I can't deal with this. It's too hard to be happy in this kind of situation.* If so, that's okay. We need to be kind to ourselves and value our own honesty.

If we're gentle with ourselves, we may even realize that we've bought into the idea that we can't be happy unless certain conditions are met, when actually, our perceptions of what will satisfy us have been strongly influenced by others.

Every day we're bombarded with advertisements that tell us our lives won't be complete unless we own this or that. The media is filled with stories of people who *seem* to be happy because they're rich celebrities, implying that money and fame are the keys to lasting joy. Our parents, families, teachers, and communities have their own ideas about what leads to happiness, and we may well discover that their formula for joy doesn't work for us. So when we finally achieve what we believe makes us happy, it could very well turn out that we're just as depressed as before. Yet when we're true to our deepest values and desires, we avoid focusing on what we don't value and instead concentrate on what we do, thus fostering our own happiness.

Happiness Begins Within

I regularly update my affirmations and express gratitude for my circumstances . . . even if they haven't yet manifested in my life. For example, I'll affirm how happy I am that I've spoken to a large audience that was receptive, warm, engaged, and inspired by my words— and I do this before I give the speech. Recently, one of my affirmations was: *I am so very glad my sister found the heirloom ring of Mom's that was misplaced.* I envisioned my sister holding the ring in her hand, with a big smile on her face, eager to call me and let me know that after all her searching, she'd found it. I felt excited, grateful, and joyous each time I imagined this . . . and wasn't at all surprised that I got a call from her a few days later letting me know that the ring had surfaced!

When you create the internal conditions for happiness within yourself, you shift into a positive emotional state, and the universe responds by matching your external circumstances. It doesn't always seem this way, but that's because you're probably not always aware of how much inner turmoil you have. If in your subconscious mind you feel sadness, the universe will attract situations to you that reflect sorrow. In this way, you get the opportunity to bring all the pain you've been unaware of to the surface and process it at last to create happiness inside of you at the deepest level. In this way, you work with the universe to create the conditions that are best for you.

All of us have healing to do, and if we make the effort to discover which of our beliefs and emotions are disempowering, we can start the healing process. It's even good to do this when our lives seem to be chugging along pretty well. While it's not smart to go *looking* for problems, we should be mindful of that little voice that says, "I'm not as happy as I could be," or "This situation isn't right for me." This voice can be very quiet, but if we don't listen to it, the universe will eventually bring our attention to it by creating a situation that makes it nearly impossible to ignore.

The following story is a good example of how a friend of mine finally decided to listen to that quiet urging in her head. She confided in me that years ago she'd gotten married out of fear. She'd been young and insecure, feeling like she'd never find someone who'd be able to accept and love her as she was, so she settled for someone who liked her a lot but always seemed to be trying to change her. For too long, my friend ignored her inner awareness that this man was not the right partner for her, but she allowed her fear of being alone prevent her from confronting the truth. It wasn't until her husband had an affair that this woman allowed her true feelings and thoughts to surface.

The good news is that because my friend could no longer ignore what she knew—or the unhappiness it was causing—she began to work on healing herself from the inside. Eventually she met, and married, someone who truly loved her for who she is. Together, they're very happy, and now she can say that she's glad her first husband's infidelity was what led her to stop running away from her heartache and start creating joy.

You Can Be Happy Even If Others Aren't

It's certainly a challenge to be upbeat when you're around people who are miserable. Their negative mood is bound to affect your own, unless you work hard at consciously maintaining more positive emotions. If you create a habit of being cheerful, you'll be less likely to slip into sorrow when you're around someone who's feeling bad . . . and you may even find that it's possible to have a sense of humor about it.

A friend of mine runs a family business with her sister, who becomes frustrated every time she isn't able to figure out a function on the computer. Every time something doesn't work the way she wants, she proceeds to curse and yell about how awful the machine is. Since they work together in the same small office, my friend is affected by her sister's outbursts of negative energy. Although they have a running joke about this, they've worked out an agreement that my friend will either ask her sister to stop working on the computer or she'll leave the room herself, because she's so sensitive to her sister's negative emotions. As she told me, "I can handle distractions, but it's like the temperature in the room changes. I just have to get out for a little while until my sister figures out the solution and goes back to being in a good mood."

Some people have thick skin when it comes to ignoring detrimental emotional energy, and some, like me, are very sensitive to it by nature. Nowadays I have such a reserve of happiness that it takes a lot to bring me down. If I'm around someone who's depressed or angry, I instantly pick up on those feelings, but I don't personalize them. I recognize that this person isn't angry because of something *I've* done, and I don't allow my own feelings to slip into negativity. I simply walk away from the person or situation, and if I can't do that, I concentrate on growing my own happiness.

Sometimes the unhappiness of others is quite intense. It can be intimidating to speak up when they're angry, but it's good to confront and alert them about what their behavior is causing. However, you must keep in mind that nothing they say in response can *make* you feel bad. You're in charge of your thoughts and feelings, and you decide what attitude you want to have. Try telling yourself something like: *I'm sorry she is so angry, but I'm not going to respond with anger to her bitterness and sharp criticisms because I choose to feel happy.* Like my friend, you may choose to just walk out of the room or avoid those people when they're in an unpleasant mood in order to hang on to your own joy.

Such an attitude can be hard to maintain when the person you're dealing with is a loved one, but you can't make *anyone* happy. All you can do is be in high spirits yourself, invite the other person to switch into a more positive emotional state, and accept the decision to remain troubled if that's what he or she chose.

Please note that some people can become so profoundly unhappy that they require professional help. It's very important to recognize the limits of your ability to pull someone out of a depression—never feel that you ought to be able to cure another's misery simply because you love that person deeply.

Happiness Comes and Goes

Happiness ebbs and flows. While you can make a conscious choice to switch your emotions and return to a happier state, it's impossible to avoid feeling unhappy at times. You can't just flip a switch and be instantly joyous, but you can make a concerted effort to lift yourself out of sadness and into bliss.

When my mother was dying, we all knew that it was only a matter of time before we'd lose her. My emotions went through peaks and valleys as I endured the process of grieving before she was even gone. There were many moments when I'd sit and cry, thinking about what we were able to do together that we'd never do again. That October, I realized we were sharing her last Thanksgiving—so even as I allowed myself to feel grief that this would be the last holiday we'd spend together, I also reminded myself to cherish the day. Therefore, I became much more aware of the good things in life than I'd normally be. It's as if each emotion were a glass of fine wine, and I was slowing down to swirl the glass, smell the bouquet, and notice all the flavors as I sipped it. I paid attention to my thoughts and feelings as I spent hours sitting with Mom and found that while I was sad, most of the time I experienced gratitude that I could have a few more moments with her.

When my mother was first admitted to the hospital, with someone from our family at her bedside around the clock, I'd wonder, *What is she feeling? Many people aren't fortunate enough to have so many of their loved ones with them at this precious time—and in fact, many don't even have a brief moment in which to say good-bye.* I'd look at her and try to understand what she was feeling. She seemed resigned, as if she were simply observing all that was going on and beginning the process of letting go.

My brother had constructed a giant collage of events in her life, and we'd all sit there and talk about the memories attached to each photograph. We made Mom's hospital room more homey by bringing in soft, pink pillows and fresh flowers, and we unconditionally shared our happiness, reminiscing about the funny times we've had.

Knowing Mom, she would have wanted our family to be happy and not keep ourselves in a state of deep sadness, so we allowed our feelings to come and go naturally. I didn't run away from my joy or my sorrow. I didn't think, *I shouldn't be happy right now; she might be offended,* or *I shouldn't be upset because it's not good to remain in sadness.* I was calm and fully present in the moment because I was accepting the rhythm of my feelings. When Mom ultimately passed away, I'd already done some of my grieving and was able to say good-bye and let her go. I know that I wouldn't have been able to do so if I'd been fighting the process and trying to guess what I *ought* to be feeling at any moment. I discovered that by submitting to this experience, even in the sad moments, beauty and joy would always return.

Living joyously—seeing with eyes of curiosity and appreciation—puts our problems in perspective. We see possibilities instead of roadblocks and hope instead of despair. I can see why people might think that happiness is the be-all and end-all, but is it? What about all the other important qualities I've embraced along the way? Was there something I'd overlooked in my zealous quest for the one thing?

Chapter Eight

THE WON THING

*"The one thing that doesn't abide by
majority rule is a person's conscience."*

— FROM *TO KILL A MOCKINGBIRD*, BY HARPER LEE

There are so many choices in life, and so much information to sort through, that it can be hard to figure out what we need in order to feel joyous, successful, and fulfilled. We're tempted to believe that there's a magic formula that will simplify all the ideas we've heard about and help us achieve complete clarity on what steps to take.

After all my searching and much introspection, I've finally found the answer to what the one thing is: There is no *one thing*. There's no absolute truth that will erase all my confusion and take away all my hurts and fears.

But the Won Thing, the winning formula, does exist. I'd like to share it with you, but you must understand that the Won Thing is unique to *you,* and it's ever changing.

What Your Won Thing Is

The Won Thing is your personal recipe for joy, satisfaction, and sense of purpose, and it combines all the elements I've talked about in this book:

- Taking responsibility for your own life

- Managing your thoughts and emotions

- Setting and achieving your goals

- Giving to others unconditionally out of a sense of personal passion

- Feeling grateful

- Attending to the small stuff and taking pride in your work

- Being happy

As you've seen, to achieve each of these elements requires you to have balance and adaptability in your life. For example, if you decide that your calling is to help those in need, you can't deplete this ambition by overextending yourself. Or if you set the goal to achieve a certain title at your company, you'll need to be willing to adjust that objective if you're moved to a different department. It's not good for your well-being to measure yourself by whether or not you've achieved all your goals exactly as you've planned; flexibility is a key component of your journey.

No one can tell you the point at which you're shifting out of equilibrium and toward the path of struggle, frustration, and unhappiness. Only *you* will be able to sense when you're giving too much or becoming mired in perfectionism. Since each individual has his or her own point of balance, the best way to find yours is to be honest with yourself about your values and listen to your feelings about what's right for you—your inner guidance won't steer you wrong.

The following story, adapted from *Aesop's Fables*, captures just what happens when you keep looking outside of yourself for the answer to how you should live your life:

The Man, the Boy, and the Donkey

There was once a man who decided to sell his donkey at the market, and he enlisted his young son to come along to help him. Together, the two of them set out for the village, walking alongside their donkey.

Soon, they passed a fellow who called out to them, "Are you traveling all the way to the village with that donkey?"

"Yes, we are," the man replied.

"Why don't you ride it? What's a donkey for if not to give you a ride? How foolish!"

The man mumbled, "Of course . . . you're right," and helped his son onto the donkey's back.

They continued on toward the market and soon passed a group of men who shouted, "Are you traveling

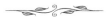
all the way to the village? Shame on you, boy, letting your poor old father walk all that way when you're young and healthy!"

Embarrassed, the man took his son off the donkey's back and got on himself.

A few miles later, the travelers came to the edge of the village. As they passed two women, the man heard one of them say to the other, "Isn't it awful? That man is making that poor child walk all the way to the village while he rides."

Flustered again, the man instructed his son to sit behind him on the donkey as they rode into town.

Soon, they came upon another group of men who said in disgust, "Look at that poor, frail donkey trying to carry two people. How terribly you're treating that animal!"

The poor farmer didn't know what to do. He was making everyone angry today! Finally, he had an idea. He asked his son to help him cut down a large tree branch and tie the donkey's feet to it with some rope, explaining, "We'll carry him upside down to the village, and then no one will criticize us for riding him or not riding him."

The boy worked with his father to tie up the donkey, who began to bray and struggle in protest. It was difficult, but they finally tied him up and hoisted the makeshift rod over their shoulders. As they began to walk over the bridge into the village, all the people in the market began to point and laugh. "What are they doing? How crazy is that man?!" they said.

The terrified donkey thrashed about so much that he kicked loose from the ropes, fell off the bridge into the water, and drowned.

An old man who had witnessed it all said, "That will teach you. Please all . . . and you please none."

The Won Thing

Everyone has an opinion, but only *you* know what the right decision is for you. When you look outside of yourself for the answers, you'll find both good and bad advice; if you try listening to everyone, you'll lose sight of what matters to you most. The solution is to work with your inner wisdom and all that you've learned to figure out your personal recipe for fulfillment and joy. In other words, to find your Won Thing, listen to your heart, mind, and body—not just to outside opinions. Only then can you come up with the unique recipe that's right for you.

What's most important to you should not be based on what others say, but on what you *know* is valuable and what you *feel* is a priority. To really identify what that is for you, you must know yourself and be completely honest so that you're sure to be loyal to your values and what you want to create in your life. This all begins with loving yourself—when you do, you'll set aside those voices that fret, "Who am I to deserve that?" "Who am I to accomplish that?" or "Who am I to feel that way?" The more you appreciate yourself, the more you'll be able to trust in your vision. With enough self-love, you can discover what you're meant to do while staying true to your goals.

Your path may take you in unexpected directions—and you may not be able to see all the way down the road—but you'll know whether or not you've made a wrong turn and recognize when you need to change directions. All will be clear to you because you have an inner compass that won't steer you wrong. By paying attention to your most cherished beliefs and honoring them, you'll know when a move isn't right. You'll have the ability to identify when you're stalling out and bravely explore why that happened, working through the roadblocks you've created in your mind and accessing your creativity and resilience.

Here's something to keep in mind: Once you think you've discovered the Won Thing that creates that sense of accomplishment and contentment you've been after, know that it may change tomorrow. The formula for fulfillment will adjust at different times in your life; for example, at one point you might be focusing on achieving your goals, but then later it may shift to a greater emphasis on being grateful for what you have. Each time you feel a yearning for something better—for greater pleasure and happiness—you can change your formula and find what works for you in that moment. When you discover it, you'll find that all you long for shows up at just the right time because you're dedicated to your passion.

Using Your Personal Recipe

You can't create your personal recipe unless you know what you're trying to make. To that end, ask yourself, "What is the purpose or guiding principle of my life?" When you can answer that question, you'll be able to easily recognize what matches up with your purpose and what doesn't. So, for whatever decision you have to make, you can ask yourself, "If I take this particular course, will it be in alignment with my purpose?" If you find that it isn't, then you know that's not the path for you. And even if it is, you should still ask yourself if there are other paths that might align with your intention as well—there might be an even better road than the one that first appeared.

The Won Thing

Think of your purpose as a dish you'd like to make and the Won Thing as the recipe. As the cook, you may have to make do without particular ingredients at times or wait until you can get different ones. It's up to you to decide if you want to place more emphasis on giving rather than attaining status or on managing your thoughts to move away from perfectionism. *You* get to decide what you're making and how you go about it.

Although you're in charge of your life and get to determine what the Won Thing is for you, you're not always going to have complete control over your circumstances. All chefs have to improvise at times, but they don't lose sight of their purpose: if they're making soup, they know they have to chop vegetables; if they're creating a dessert, they leave the vegetables aside and begin whipping the cream.

Pinpointing your aspirations may take time—it took me years to recognize that mine is to make a positive contribution to the lives of others. If I'm offered an opportunity to do something that doesn't fit my purpose, and I'm indecisive about turning it down, I'll wonder, *Why would I want to do this when it doesn't seem to fit into my purpose?* Very often, the answer is rooted in deeply hidden beliefs that need to be healed, such as: *Because I'm afraid of what will happen if I don't,* or *Because I feel I have to prove my worth.*

Old, negative ideologies can be so ingrained in our minds that we have to work quite hard to erase them. Every time we do, they become more faint and less likely to influence us. The only way to totally eliminate them, though, is to recognize when they're affecting us and consciously choose to replace them with healthier sentiments that are in alignment with our ultimate destination.

The reason so many of us don't know our ambitions is because we're often not encouraged to discover what will give us a sense of meaning and fulfillment. Most of us have been taught to live our lives a certain way and told that if we come across any problems, we should work hard to fix them so that we can get back to how life should be. We think, according to this framework, that we'll be happy most of the time. But if we're not aligned to our purpose and try to conform to someone else's idea of what will fulfill us, we'll lose sight of what we value and experience frustration when problems won't go away. Even if we follow someone else's formula for happiness and our problems are minimal, we're likely to be dissatisfied and wonder, *Is this all there is?*

We're the only ones who can figure out what our own purpose is or what will keep us connected to the passions and yearnings of our own heart and soul. Our direction isn't necessarily something grand or predetermined; we don't arrive on this planet with a single, unalterable mission. I think it's up to us to decide what our design is, and we'll feel grounded and secure once we do. On some level—due to that inner compass—we sense that this is the case, and that's why we long to discover why we're here.

Your purpose may not be tied to serving others, but if you're living whatever *it* is, it's hard not to affect others for the better . . . and you might never even be aware that you are. Like George Bailey in the movie *It's a Wonderful Life,* you could overlook the many times in your life where you made a decision to do the right thing and live according to your values, profoundly affecting the lives of others.

Grounded by Your Purpose

Having a sense of purpose is knowing that what you're doing at any time is in perfect alignment with who you are, your values, and visions—which gives you grounding and guidance.

Recently, I went into an upscale men's clothing store to get gifts for my son, Michel, and husband, Denis. The salesman clearly loved what he did, because he greeted me like this: "So tell me, what are your needs today and how can I help you fulfill them?"

That question took me by surprise, since it wasn't what I'm used to hearing when I walk into a store. Instead of responding, "Just looking," as I usually do, I explained exactly why I was there, because I felt that this man genuinely wanted to assist me in achieving my goal. I said, "I have to get my son some clothes for my mom's funeral, and being a teenager, he's very particular about what he wears. I really want to make sure I buy something that he can wear again, although he's still growing. And I also want to buy a new outfit for my husband, but he's particular about what he wears, too."

The salesman started by showing me pairs of pants for Michel, describing why they fit the bill. He even stopped me from buying a particular wallet, explaining why it wasn't the best one for my son. By the time I left, I had exactly what I'd been looking for. I told him, "You know, you're really good at what you do." He responded, "Thanks! I feel better knowing that I met your needs."

If the salesman's purpose had been to sell as many high-priced articles as he could, he wouldn't have been so effective. What's more, I might have left the store frustrated that I'd spent too much money on items that

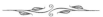
weren't right for Michel and Denis. While this employ-ee's objective at work may have been to sell clothing, my guess is that he was clear on his life's purpose, which allowed him to do his job without trying to manipulate people into opening their wallets and buying whatever would get him the highest commission.

When we live according to our purpose, we experience joy, generosity, trust, and curiosity. We naturally attract the means to achieve our goals and have clarity about how to move forward—life is as it was meant to be.

So what's your personal recipe, your Won Thing? The answer is in the final chapters of this book.

PART II

MAKING THE WON THING WORK FOR YOU

Chapter Nine

ALIGNING
WITH YOUR
PURPOSE

"Nobody can teach what is inside a person;
it has to be discovered for oneself and
a way must be found to express it."

— EDUARDO CHILLIDA

Most of us simply react to the problems we encounter instead of focusing on enjoying life, creating positive feelings, and trusting that we can envision a fulfilling existence for ourselves—ultimately discovering our Won Thing. We must let go of the distractions that keep us running from here to there and set aside time for reflection—whether that means going on a retreat or vacation, meditating, journaling, or taking a long walk. Allowing ourselves to step back and think about where

our lives are headed gives us a chance to check in with our feelings and discover—or rediscover—what matters most to us; it's our opportunity to examine our inner compass.

Often, but not always, a sense of purpose results when we use our gifts to make a difference in the world. When we help others, we become acutely aware that there are people who care about us and are able to count on us. We'll feel better about ourselves—and hopeful, too—because we'll see the positive contribution we're making. But how can we know what our gifts even are, let alone how we might bring them to light, if we're so busy that we never stop to wonder, *Why am I here?* or *How might I serve?*

As I've said, your purpose doesn't have to be grand. It might simply be to live a happy life, bring joy to the people you care about, and be a good person. But how *you* define "happy life" and "good person" won't necessarily be how *I* define them—we both have our own values, and there's nothing wrong with that. When you take the time to discover what truly matters to *you,* you'll start to discover what your personal Won Thing is.

First, do a little research on yourself: Do you need to be around people and deeply involved in others' lives? Do you feel that you're living out your purpose by spending long hours doing research that may lead to great scientific breakthroughs? Do you need to connect to your spirit every day through prayer and meditation? Or do you experience your spirituality simply by interacting with others in a positive way?

As you think about activities that have meaning for you, never minimize the ways in which you accomplish your goals. Don't be too quick to listen to others

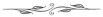

who think less of you because you didn't operate in the way they did or express yourself in a particular way—people may not even realize that they're hurting your feelings when they're critical of how you live your life. Sometimes they're so focused on the formula for success they've been taught to follow that they respond negatively whenever someone contradicts it. They may not even know what their Won Thing is, so they certainly won't recognize that your recipe is going to be true to your own unique feelings, beliefs, and values. It's important to always remember that there's more than one way to be spiritual, give in service to others, or do anything in life.

The Seven Parts to the Winning Formula

In Part I of this book, you learned about seven parts that make up the winning formula for fulfillment, success, and happiness. You discovered the upside of each and the downside of focusing too much on specific elements as if they represented the ultimate solution. In the process, you realized that your formula must be your personal way of finding balance in life while utilizing these seven qualities.

What follows is a summary of the topics covered in the first seven chapters, in order to illustrate the harmony that's necessary as you work toward your Won Thing:

1. Rescue. You can't look to anyone else to rescue you from your unhappiness. At the same time, you're not an island and there will be situations when you need to

lean on others for support. Balance means finding that middle ground between trying to do everything yourself and expecting others to do it all for you.

2. Managing your thoughts and emotions. No one else can *make* you feel happy or sad, since you're the one who chooses your emotions and the thoughts that support them. The more positive your feelings and beliefs are, the better your circumstances will be—but avoiding your negative emotions and thoughts altogether isn't healthy. You have to allow them to arise so that you can learn from them, and then you must let them fade as you replace them with more positive sentiments. Balance means doing your inner work along with your outer work, attending to your mind-set and emotions, and, at the same time, acting positively. It will be easier to motivate yourself when you're feeling good, but you do have to act. If you get stuck analyzing and find that you're not moving forward—or you simply feel good, enjoying your emotions but never acting on them—you aren't in balance.

3. Being goal and achievement oriented. Moving forward, step-by-step, toward your goals is important for achieving what you desire. However, there are times when you need to be in a state of quiet receptivity, remaining in one place as you open up to new ideas and possibilities and trusting that they'll come to you.

4. Giving to others. By balancing giving and receiving, you're able to do good in the world without becoming depleted and burned out.

5. Feeling gratitude. It's important to accept your situation as it is in this moment, learn what you can from it, and find reasons to be grateful. At the same time, you probably want to create something better for yourself. Balance means finding common ground between striving and accepting.

6. Attending to the details. If you want to achieve your goals, you have to cross your *T*'s and dot your *I*'s and take pride in doing your best at what matters most to you. However, you don't want to fall into perfectionism and become so bogged down by details that you lose track of your priorities.

7. Being happy. Although you might aspire to be happy all the time, you have to accept that as long as you're part of the human race, you'll never achieve that goal. Balance means accepting the natural ebb and flow of your emotions and learning from your difficulties so that you can let go of them and return to a state of joy.

Everyone has a different state of equilibrium, and at any given moment, you're probably not in perfect symmetry in every area. Balance happens over time, and the elements that make up an attuned relationship or person are constantly changing. For example, a marriage should truly be a 50-50 partnership, but sometimes one spouse gives 70 percent while the other is giving 30 percent; and other times one is giving 95 percent while the other is giving 5. Both partners switch back and forth from giving support to receiving it so that over the course of the marriage, it's an equal union.

People are always working to balance their personal and professional lives, focusing on both their families

and themselves. When you know what your purpose and priorities are, you'll have an easier time achieving that perfect proportion. By regularly setting aside time for reflection and developing the habit of introspection, you can ensure that you'll bring yourself back into harmony whenever you fall out of it.

When You Fall Out of Balance

If you're constantly reacting to life or letting other people and outside circumstances rearrange your goals, you'll lose your sense of direction, and your priorities will become mixed up. Know what your purpose is and reflect on it often so that you can live in alignment with your winning recipe for success—the Won Thing that will bring the joy and contentment you seek.

To make sure I stay balanced and true to my priorities —finding a happy medium between doing and having done for me—I carefully organize my time. I don't want to suddenly find myself thinking, *What am I doing with my life? How did I get here, and where am I going?* I want to spend time feeling gratitude for all of my blessings and focusing on what I want to create for myself each precious day. I remain mindful and correct my course if I start spending too much time on something that's taking me away from my purpose.

For example, if it's 5 P.M. and I suddenly realize that I've been working so much that I haven't said more than two sentences to my husband all day, I almost always make the conscious choice to shut off my computer. It's important for me to have time with my husband and son so that I feel completely present in the moment.

So, when I realize that I haven't interacted with them enough, I end my workday. And if I'm at the dinner table sharing a meal with my family, I manage my thoughts and stop myself from daydreaming about what I'm going to do tomorrow. Believe me, it took a long time and a lot of effort to bring my life more into balance—it's not easy to break mindless habits.

Sometimes, of course, I'm on a roll with a task and stay logged on to the Internet far past dinnertime. The difference is that when I do so, I'm usually making a conscious choice. If I were to automatically brush aside my awareness that I was pulling myself out of balance, working too many hours would become a deeply ingrained habit. Soon I'd find myself living a life very different from the one I worked so hard to create for myself. So I make my choice: I try not to waste time feeling guilty or second-guessing myself, and I remain aware of my need to bring myself back into balance by making a healthier choice tomorrow. Although I'm not 100 percent in balance at all times—no one is—that's what I always aim for.

The following exercises can help you create harmony by using the power of your emotions. Listen to your instincts about which scenarios you'd like to create in your mind and the feelings you'd like to generate. You and only you know deep down if you're too focused on the details, spending too much time in negativity, looking to others for rescue when you have the capacity to solve your own problems, and so on. Read through these exercises slowly, and then give them a try.

Exercise 1: Creating Positive Emotions Using Your Memory

Think back to a time when you did any of the following:

- Rescued yourself

- Let someone else take care of you

- Consciously managed your thoughts and emotions

- Stopped analyzing your thoughts and emotions and simply did what you knew needed to be done

- Pushed past an obstacle and went on to achieve a particular goal

- Allowed yourself time to slow down so you could discover what your next step should be, and then the wisdom came to you

- Gave from the heart in service to others, and it felt right

- Took time to nurture and replenish yourself after giving to others

- Expressed genuine gratitude

- Felt a deep desire to create something even better than what you had

- Attended to the details of a certain task and achieved positive results

- Made the decision to let go of some of the details of a task and then focused on the bigger picture

- Truly felt happy

- Had a deep insight or revelation as a result of listening to what your painful feelings taught you

Replay the scenes in your mind. Remember the way you felt, and savor those feelings.

Exercise 2: Creating Positive Emotions Using Your Imagination

Choose one of the following thoughts, and embellish it by creating a corresponding scene in your imagination that allows you to generate positive emotions.

Think of:	Imagine a scene in which you:
• A problem you're struggling with	• Solve the problem on your own
• A painful emotion you're experiencing	• Are experiencing a more positive emotion
• A goal you want to reach	• Take action by working toward a goal and then finally achieving it
• Someone you'd like to help or a cause you'd like to contribute to in some way	• Help a person or contribute to a cause in a way that makes a real difference in the lives of others
• Something you'd like to have in your life	• Are genuinely experiencing deep gratitude for all you have and for having attained what you desire
• A situation where you feel anxious about getting the details right	• Are focusing on the big picture, and all the details are being taken care of without your having to worry or struggle
• A situation that would make you feel happy	• Are experiencing a profound sense of joy

Make the scene in your mind as real as it can be. Feel the emotions as if this situation were the real thing and not an imaginary exercise.

Downtime and Reflection

Where I live in Canada, I often have the chance to take very long drives. I love a lengthy car ride because it gives me an opportunity to get away from distractions and reflect. These opportunities to get away and think are very important to me because I find that if I don't check in within, I can become stressed out and even develop an illness—which is a sign of imbalance.

Living according to your purpose means having a vision. A lack of direction leads to dashing here and there—putting out fires and trying to solve problems— but not knowing where you're going or why you want to go there. By allowing yourself some downtime, you start to become more reflective, which lets you gain perspective, recharge your batteries, and correct your course.

Although I've had a lot of wonderful jobs in my life, there's one early in my career that I was fired from. While it's an awful feeling to be told "This isn't working out," after I packed up my office and drove home, I had a chance to think about what had just happened, and I had to admit that the job was a bad fit. Several people had highly recommended the company to me because it was supposedly *the* place to work. My gut had told me it wasn't right for me, however, particularly since I felt that the firm was very behind, technologically. I knew that I wouldn't feel proud to work there, which is important to me.

Despite the red flags, I listened to others and applied for a job writing manuals for their new, inferior equipment. I wasn't selling it, so I convinced myself to overcome my negative feelings about the products, the job, and the company, and to just fill up the hours from nine to five and collect my paycheck (it did pay well). Even so, I hated every minute of it! I had a dark, cramped, windowless office in the back of the building that felt like a prison cell where I was doing hard time. Because of my attitude, I didn't do my best and couldn't bring myself to care—I would have fired me, too! But at the time, I didn't have the self-esteem to say, "I deserve a job that's the right fit for me, one that makes me feel inspired to rush in to the office each morning and start another exciting day."

When I became unemployed, I looked at it as an opportunity to pull myself back from fearful and reactive behaviors. So, as difficult as it was to let go of my fears about money and having a hole on my résumé that future employers would ask me about, I knew I had to stop worrying about the opinions of others and start consulting my inner compass.

I asked myself what I wanted and needed, and then focused on the type of job that would fit into my picture of a life that was happy, fulfilling, exciting, rewarding, and filled with abundance. I took a look at how I'd compromised on values that were important in order to get hired and how that had made me feel. And while I still remember how shocked, embarrassed, and scared I was at that time in my life, I'm grateful I had that opportunity to discover for myself the importance of considering my purpose before making big decisions. Since then, I have been very clear on what the Won Thing is for me. It changes here and there—when I became a parent, for instance, my ideas of what I wanted my life to look like shifted a lot—but my core values have always determined my personal recipe.

It has become my passion to help others find their *own* passion, as well as assisting them in exploring the

many elements they can incorporate into their personal Won Thing. In the past, I've coached people one-on-one, and now I write and teach folks how to market their books and develop greater happiness. I feel peaceful yet enthusiastic, because I know that I'm living in accordance with my unique set of values and desires.

From Mindlessness to Mindfulness

I once had a dentist who tried to get me to floss my teeth daily, stressing the importance of flossing and how it prevents gingivitis, which not only leads to losing your teeth but to diabetes and heart disease as well. I took her warning seriously, but somehow I kept forgetting to follow her advice since it just wasn't my habit. Then, on my next visit, she gave me a handful of dental-floss dispensers and said, "I want you to put one out on your sink—not in the medicine cabinet, but on the sink where you can see it. Put one in your purse, one in your car, and put the others anywhere you'll regularly see the floss and remember to use it." I took her advice (and her freebies), and sure enough, I almost immediately developed the habit of flossing regularly. I wasn't able to get away from the dental floss because it was always there, reminding me of my goal.

In the same way that I learned to floss habitually, I shifted from only stating affirmations when I was getting ready in the morning to repeating them often during the day. I printed them out and started putting them everywhere: in my purse, in my car, on my nightstand, by the bathroom mirror, next to my computer, and on the door of my refrigerator. At a stoplight, I'd look at the list of affirmations I kept in my car and say them aloud, generating the powerful emotions connected with these positive thoughts. I'd even pull the list out of my purse and silently read them in the waiting room at the doctor's office. When I would open the refrigerator and gather ingredients to make a meal, there the list would be, right in my face. Each time I came across my affirmations or had a moment to glance at them, I did so. In this way, I didn't just feel great and optimistic ten minutes during my morning routine; I felt those emotions throughout the day.

The results were amazing. You see, when I was just working with affirmations and feeling great for a small amount of time once a day, I wasn't making a big difference in my overall emotional state. Ninety percent of the time, I was worrying, feeling bad about myself, or thinking about my problems and how awful they were, so this small amount of constructive thinking couldn't counteract so much negative energy—no wonder they weren't working! When I developed the habit of using these powerful statements more frequently, I was soon feeling good instead of bad 90 percent of the time.

Establishing the *habit* of positivity allows you to remember that you want to be in balance and that your thoughts and emotions are under your control. Soon, you'll be noticing when your thinking turns detrimental and immediately switch to: *Can I learn from what I'm feeling here? Or is this emotion the result of habitual negative thinking?* If you can learn from it, great; sit with it and explore it. Otherwise, switch out of it immediately. Having experienced your ability to create a more beneficial outlook simply by changing your thoughts, you'll know that you can do it right now by letting go of that dark feeling and bringing in joyful notions.

So while there's no simple answer that allows everyone to create fulfillment and happiness, you, like everyone else, can discover your Won Thing. There's a simple formula for breaking down the sometimes intimidating task of meeting your overarching goal of pleasure and contentment, and you'll learn about it next.

Chapter Ten

THE THREE-STEP PROCESS FOR CREATING YOUR WINNING FORMULA

"The creation of a thousand forests is in one acorn."

— RALPH WALDO EMERSON

While traveling recently, I stopped to have dinner at a Chinese buffet that claimed to have more than 100 items on the menu. I figured that with so many choices, I'd definitely find something delicious to eat. But as I looked over the buffet, I discovered that most of the dishes were either swimming in gravy or oil, or were deep-fried. Since that's not the type of meal I was looking for, I soon realized that my options weren't as plentiful as I'd expected.

If you're in the process of deciding what you want for yourself—and you're looking for advice, guidance,

and information—you may feel overwhelmed at first, but then you'll realize that your choices are as abundant as a 100-item buffet. The sheer number of them may seem like too much to consider, but as you look more carefully, you'll start to sort through those choices and quickly eliminate the ones that aren't right for you.

It's only natural that we respond to so much information and so many options by wishing for the one thing that would solve all of our problems and lead to success, fulfillment, and contentment. Life would be much simpler if there were something out there that was always guaranteed to work, but one size doesn't fit all.

Even those handy hints you can get on the Internet or in magazines may not be appropriate for you. For example, I once came across a list of tips for losing weight that included "Never eat after 8:00 P.M.," which would be hard to do if you had a job where you worked until 7:30. Another tip advised putting a photo of yourself at your heaviest weight on the refrigerator to discourage you from snacking . . . but I've also heard that you should put a photo of yourself looking your thinnest and most fit on your refrigerator for inspiration. Contradictory advice is everywhere. The best dieting tip I probably ever heard was: "Eat less, mostly vegetables." Wouldn't it be great if every dilemma in life could be solved so simply? But actually, even *that* advice isn't so simple. Should you cook the vegetables or eat them raw? If you eat less, does that mean less food altogether, or just fewer calories or junk foods? And shouldn't you actually increase your intake of items that are full of nutrients and fiber? I could go on and on.

While you may crave simple answers, unfortunately they're rare. You may be able to find some general guidance that makes sense to you, but what's the best process for sorting through all of the overwhelming opinions and figuring out what works for *you?* I believe in following the three-step approach of *sort, match up,* and *modify.*

<u>Sort</u> *Through Information and Potential Choices*

The first step in sorting through huge amounts of information and potential choices is to slow down and listen to your instincts—you see, there's a reason why you were drawn to this book and not another, and why you're attracted to one potential romantic partner and not another. If you're feeling good about yourself and confident that you'll make the right choices, you'll have less trouble with the sorting process. You'll be able to listen to your gut and go in a certain direction instead of second-guessing yourself or calling your friends and making your decision according to what they say.

Whenever people start to tell me about all of the contradictory advice they've been given, I ask them to stop for a moment and listen to what their instincts say. It's amazing how often they know what they want to do but think that they *should* check out all their other options. Often, this inability to separate out what is and isn't right is rooted in negative feelings such as fear, guilt, and low self-worth. If my clients don't trust that they can make the right decision, they'll avoid making one at all. If they don't feel good about themselves, they won't honor their desires and passions, and they'll look for the choice that they think others will approve of— but when they do, they're likely to take the wrong road for them.

If you are trying to avoid making a decision, are overwhelmed by all the possibilities, or are longing for someone to help you simplify your thought process, stop and identify what you're feeling. Generate positive emotions such as love, faith, and confidence; once you do, you'll find that it's easier to see which choices aren't right and focus on those that suit you.

Curiosity is also a positive emotion because it opens you up to a wide range of possibilities. When you go into a large bookstore, for instance, you may feel excited about all the volumes on the shelves and tables and be eager to start checking them out. Even if the number of choices makes you feel overwhelmed and confused at first, if you listen to your gut, you'll know what section of the store to gravitate toward and which books to pick up. Let your instinct guide you, because if you only listen to your head, you're likely to overlook the influence of any negative subconscious beliefs, such as: *People like me don't read about stuff like that, so I'm not going to walk into that section—someone might stare at me,* or *I really ought to be reading books on this subject even though I'm not at all inspired to do so.*

Follow your instincts whenever you're confronted by a range of choices, and then let your mind chime in with its ideas. Decisions that are in alignment with your true self are never wrong, even if they lead to situations that cause you to learn difficult lessons. Your head and gut, working together, will help you settle on which selections are good possibilities and those that you can disregard.

Match Up Your Wealth of Choices with Your Inner Desires

The next step in creating your winning formula for fulfillment, happiness, and success is to go deeper into your self-awareness so that you can identify those values, desires, and talents of yours that can be too easily overlooked. You can't know what choice to make unless you know what *you* want.

In my many years of encouraging people to achieve their goals and dream big, I've discovered that most have a sort of amnesia about all of the wondrous gifts they possess. For example, not long ago I had a client who was a dream to work with. He followed my suggestions by immediately acting upon his decision to achieve the next goal in his plan, and constantly thanked me for all that I was doing for him. What he didn't realize is that I was only pointing out to him what I perceived were his most obvious skills and talents. He had never taken the time to examine what his strengths were and hadn't actually considered himself a hard worker, yet that was my main impression of him!

You may have noticed something similar with someone you care about, because people so often underestimate themselves. When they're feeling scared, vulnerable, or insecure, they'll totally forget the marvelous things they've accomplished, which I think is due to so many folks not receiving a lot of praise in the early stages of their lives. You were probably scolded or criticized when you did something wrong, but how often did your parents, teachers, relatives, or older siblings congratulate you for doing something right? You may have begun to take your skills, talents, and positive characteristics for

granted . . . until they eventually dropped out of your conscious perception of who you are.

Part of being reflective is taking the time to notice what you do right. Did you treat your children well as you drove them to school today? Did you handle a conflict with a peer by starting a healthy and productive dialogue? Did you use your creativity to solve a problem?

Also take note of what you've done in the past that was positive and admirable. What talents do you have that you've forgotten? I'm always fascinated to learn that someone I know has an interesting past, having triumphed over a huge challenge or mastered a valuable skill. As you identify the gifts that you've been overlooking, you'll find that you've discovered tools you can use to achieve your personal goals.

It's helpful to have a friend, coach, therapist, or peer who's able to remind us of our positive qualities, since we so often only look at ourselves one way. Not long ago, my sister bought me a makeup mirror that allows me to change the lighting to see what I look like in daylight, indoors, or at night; and I can flip it over to see my face magnified five times. I never realized how much different I look when the light changes or when I'm peering closely at myself. We often aren't even aware that the way we see ourselves is much different from the way others perceive us.

While it's beneficial for others to remind us of our worthy characteristics, it's also helpful for neutral parties to point out any contradictions between what we say our values are and the choices we're making. While this may not be easy for us to hear, it's important that we do. We need to be as aware as possible when weighing choices— our decisions should always be made consciously so that they resonate with who we truly are.

When It's Hard to Make a Choice

When you're feeling panicked about making a choice, the tendency is to do it quickly so you can then relax and shift into a more peaceful state. If you approach a crisis or problem in this way, however, you're likely to make the wrong decision. You see, you can't access your inner wisdom until you first become calm and have faith in yourself—only *then* will you have an inner awareness of which path to take.

One of the reasons why we sometimes panic and come to quick conclusions is because we're uncomfortable in the moment. Here's an example from my own life: I find the province we're currently living in to be a challenge because I don't speak the French language and it's very difficult to find a doctor here. Denis and I have made the decision to move after Michel graduates from high school, but I've already been doing Internet research on neighborhoods and looking at houses for sale. I know that when we get closer to that time, we'll find the right place; even so, I've been feeling particularly anxious about moving, so I keep having the urge to call up a real-estate agent and take the steps toward buying a new house *now*.

Fortunately, I have two good friends who know me well—whenever I call them to say, "Hey, I found a great house in Ontario and I'm thinking that maybe I should check it out just in case," they gently remind me that this would not be in keeping with my personal, winning formula at this time in my life. Part of me wants them to say, "You're right, Peggy, it *is* a fabulous house. Forget your plans . . . I think you guys should move right now!" But then again, if they did tell me that, they wouldn't be

such great friends. I'm thankful to have people in my life who will stop me from making rash decisions by pointing out that I'm acting out of alignment with the Won Thing that's unique to me.

Sometimes we just don't like the choices in front of us at the moment: I don't want to stay where I am, but I don't want to move yet, either, because it would take Michel out of his school and away from his friends. I know that in time, circumstances will change, and I'll have different options, but since the present situation isn't ideal, it *feels* as if nothing will never happen. I know that instead of focusing on what I don't have, I need to be aware of what I *do* have and feel gratitude and happiness right now.

Modify the Won Thing as Your Needs and Desires Change

The Won Thing changes over time because life changes—and so do you. In fact, modifying your winning formula according to the shifts you make on the inside—creating a new mix of elements that works for you—is something you'll do throughout your life.

When feelings of dissatisfaction creep in, it's a sure sign that you need to reassess your Won Thing. Maybe you've always loved traveling for your career but now want to settle down. Maybe you're feeling that you've been too focused on fixing the problems in your life and haven't spent enough time simply enjoying all its blessings. Or it could be that you want to devote more time to building financial wealth now or giving back to the community. If you're aware that it's time for a change,

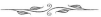

it's very important to focus on creating positive feelings so that you'll know how to adjust your personal formula for fulfillment, joy, and success.

People often become unhappy when they need to alter their Won Thing, because they're afraid to make changes. They can become fearful and pessimistic. Unable to see the possibilities for creating better situations for themselves, they only focus on all the obstacles blocking them from happiness. Yet as soon as they create more joy, they can start to see ways around those roadblocks, since positive emotions trigger our creativity.

There are countless ways for people to use their resourcefulness to initiate opportunities for self-gratification. For example, I teach people how to make money online. The way I see it, the Internet provides limitless opportunities for using the imagination to create wealth through selling products, services, and information. The World Wide Web gives my clients access to customers all over the globe, along with all sorts of portals to help them find the ones who would be most likely to respond to their particular message or products. I see many of the Web's possibilities because I actively choose to foster my own positive emotions, which puts me in a very creative state.

Now, I realize that it can be easy to buy into the notion that your current circumstances will never improve, but that's simply not true. *Everything* changes. You must ask yourself, "Do I want to react to changes that are imposed on me or take charge and create the life I want for myself?" Keep in mind that doors open and close, but at least one of them is always open somewhere. So if one shuts on you, access your curiosity and confidence so that you can persevere in discovering a new opportunity.

You might discover that your customer base has dwindled or people's needs have changed, you've relocated to an area where the circumstances for achieving your goals aren't quite as obvious and abundant, or your financial situation has changed. All of these will affect your Won Thing, of course, but try to remain confident. Your winning formula will always be based in your core values, and sometimes you just have to take a step back and look for new openings. And be patient as you work to discover new avenues, because ideas won't always come to you immediately.

Obviously, you're not who you were yesterday, the day before, 5 years ago, or 20 years ago . . . and you won't be the same in the future. Yet people tend to forget this, often fearfully locking themselves into a limiting definition of who they are and clinging to it for dear life. For instance, insisting that you're just not the type of person who can do that offers a false sense of security. Are you *sure* you're not that "type of person"? Exploring whether you may in fact have what it takes to achieve your goal is exciting and energizing if you remain in a creative state and open to possibilities.

Sometimes what you need in order to create the life you want are the skills and talents you already have but have been overlooking. Then again, what's standing between you and the life you want may simply be fear. Change often requires you to give up something, whether big or small, although you'll most likely gain something as a result. For example, although you might have to give up some money, time, or sense of comfort to achieve your Won Thing, think of what you'll be creating for yourself!

Never sacrifice your deeply held dreams and values. You do *not* have to compromise your integrity to make

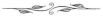

money or hide who you really are in order to find a romantic partner. When you stay true to yourself and follow the process of *sort, match up,* and *modify*—always generating positive feelings and thoughts—the circumstances of your life will begin to align with your intentions.

Checking in with Your Feelings

As I conclude this chapter, I want to stress that whenever you're trying to decide if something is in alignment with your purpose or your Won Thing, take a moment to reflect, and check in with your gut. Do you need to change your emotional state from negative to positive? In other words, you may know exactly what to do, but perhaps you first need to build up your confidence and self-love so that you can find the courage to begin moving forward. If you're afraid of the unexpected changes that might occur as you start to head in a different direction, reflection will allow you to discover that. For example, if you decide to change careers, go back to school, or relocate to another area, it's going to affect some of your relationships. If you're too afraid to explore the effects of your transitions, you'll either move forward in denial or avoid making a change altogether.

When you're contemplative, you become aware of your initial response to your goal and the changes you'll be making, since your emotions are a valuable source of information. If you feel very excited, you're probably about to embark on the right course for you. Even so, you have to keep checking in with your feelings. Are you truly excited, or are you talking yourself into being enthusiastic because you think you should be? Are you worked up but

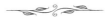

at the same time a little scared? If so, explore that feeling of fear, because sometimes it's just a brain blip that's rooted in an old belief. Go ahead and take a look at that belief—consciously and bravely—and don't be surprised if it doesn't have anything to teach you, as it could just be clutter that you need to get rid of.

Being nervous about a change doesn't mean it's not right for you. For example, you may decide that you need to develop a new skill in order to reach your goal and, being enthusiastic, you immediately hire someone to teach it to you. Then, once you begin your instruction, you start feeling uncomfortable because you encounter some old ideas about what you're not good at, or the instructor is simply not the right one for you. By exploring those beliefs that are connected to your fears and insecurities, you can definitely learn something.

In fact, you might realize that the actual lesson you were supposed to glean from this experience is not what you thought. Maybe, because of your insecurities, you're too quick to trust someone who impresses you for the wrong reasons, since you realize that the teacher you hired doesn't know how to effectively teach what you need to learn. Thanks to this experience, you're now very clear on what you're looking for, and you go on to hire the perfect instructor for you. Whatever your discomfort is, consider that it might have something to teach you, because revelations and insights often arise from listening to your instincts and feelings. As long as you learn from your missteps, they weren't taken in vain. Sometimes the wrong path leads you in the very direction you're meant to go!

Whatever path you take, you won't walk it alone, because you'll always need assistance from others who

support you in various ways. In the next chapter, you'll learn how working with other people is an important part of your winning formula, your Won Thing.

Chapter Eleven

WORKING WITH OTHERS TO CREATE THE LIFE YOU DESIRE

"Giving connects two people, the giver and the receiver, and this connection gives birth to a new sense of belonging."

— DEEPAK CHOPRA

None of us can reach our goals by ourselves, because we're all connected and require the help of others. Unfortunately, we let our fears and insecurities stop us from asking for or accepting the assistance we need. Too often, we're wary of people who are unlike us and slow to trust that they can assist us. We don't realize that while we may seem very different on the surface, we have many of the same values and desires; we just might disagree on how to achieve goals or interact with others.

Whatever our Won Thing is, the way to happiness, fulfillment, and success is not a lonely, deserted road. We'll meet many people along the way, and the more accepting and compassionate we are—not only toward them but toward ourselves—the more willing we'll be to receive and offer help on our journey.

Different Strokes

We all have different talents and interests that lead to different sets of priorities. For example, I have little interest in investments, but Denis knows that this doesn't mean I don't care about protecting our wealth. It's just that I prefer to have a general grasp on how we're investing and leave the details up to him and our money manager. My husband and I "get" each other, and there's a mutual understanding that we simply have some contrasting concerns. Frankly, I'm more intent on finding ways to generate a higher income than in being involved in the many different types of investing.

Whether you're dealing with co-workers, business partners, family members, or neighbors, know that they probably have a different recipe for success than you do—and don't assume that they don't care about yours. For instance, if you feel that you're giving more than your spouse is, you may feel that he's not supporting you. However, he might not feel that saying, "I love you" or being affectionate is important—his way of giving may be to earn a good living, which does support you and your children.

You have to remember that some people feel that simply working hard to achieve a goal but rarely expressing

themselves is acceptable, while others believe that communication between all team members is very important for the happiness and well-being of everyone involved, as well as for setting clear priorities. So whenever you perceive a difference of opinion when working with others, be curious and try to see the world through their eyes. Ask them why they do what they do, and listen to their answer. Be accepting of their viewpoint, and don't take it personally if they don't share all of your opinions and values. Seek common ground, and you'll discover that the distance between you isn't so great after all.

Ask, and You Shall Receive

I believe strongly in networking because most people are eager to help others and want to feel needed and important; so being asked to give advice, offer insights, or assist those who are on the same path but may not be quite as far along gives them a chance to experience the joy of giving.

I didn't have contacts in publishing when I started writing books a few years back, but I trusted that there were those who would want to give me a hand, and I worked hard to meet successful authors. I made it easy for them to help me, asking them for no more than I needed and being respectful of their time. By the same token, the Internet-marketing program that I currently teach focuses on finding marketing partners for authors. The greatest challenge isn't that no one will *help* my clients, but rather that too many want to!

Thanks to the Internet, it's possible to connect with just about anyone in the world. I'm old enough to

remember when, if I wanted to contact someone, I had to dial an old rotary phone and hope someone picked up on the other end, because there was no voice mail and answering machines were rare. Yet somehow people found others who could partner with them in business back in those days.

Even in these technologically advanced times, if you're looking for excuses as to why you can't reach people, you'll find them; but if your goals are rooted in passion, you'll find a way to make meaningful contacts. If you're reluctant to reach out to those you don't know or aren't very familiar with, find something in common to build a rapport with them. You can also think about what you can do for *them*. Can you brighten their day? Do them a favor? Or make it as easy as possible for them to help you?

Very often, the real reason people hesitate in asking for help isn't because they're unable to find other men and women who might be able to assist them, but because they fear that their request will be an imposition that creates resentment. Don't be afraid to ask for help; just be respectful, polite, and clear about what you want. People can always just say no, and you're not responsible for their feelings. If you ask them to give you information or do something for you, it's their responsibility to let you know if they're willing to do it. If they are, they'll tell you whether they expect to be compensated for their assistance.

Never take it upon yourself to feel bad if people give you more than they feel comfortable giving. They may feel that they already donated too much to others and are in need of a break, but they gave to you out of habit. Or maybe they weren't being honest with themselves

about their priorities, which has left them feeling bitter. None of this is your fault.

Naturally, you don't want to ask too much of someone and give the impression that you're not appreciative. Of course, if you're coming from a place of wanting to give unconditionally, you won't demand too much, be lazy, or ask for something that's really your responsibility. In fact, when you ask, "How would I go about doing that?" from a place of gratitude, the other person may very well say, "Well, I'll do it for you." You might be very surprised by his generosity!

As long as your request comes from kindness and confidence rather than scarcity, fear, insecurity, and jealousy, you won't be imposing on others. A professional I know says that when potential clients seem to have a lot of victim stories to tell, she steers clear of taking them on. From experience, she knows that these people are out of balance and are likely to see their interactions through the "martyr lens," causing them to be suspicious and distrustful. When her clients feel good about themselves, however, they're open to her suggestions and far more inclined to give and receive from the heart.

Just Say Yes to Receiving Help

When you're in a positive emotional state—living according to the Won Thing—you're able to delegate to others when it's necessary. I've had employees who didn't perform tasks exactly the way I did, but I was still grateful to have someone there to get the work done. Recently, a woman I'd hired generated a press release that I decided to make a lot of changes to. She was very apologetic that

she hadn't come closer to my vision of how it should read, but I pointed out that she'd saved me a lot of time by writing the first version, and I expressed my gratitude for her hard work and diligence. I know that it will take time for her to learn to compose drafts that are closer to how I'd like them to read, so I'm patient with her. I've been able to loosen my grip and acknowledge that others see things differently, so I'm able to see the great value in the work my employee does—and her unique approach to the task. While I decided that my method was better in this case, acknowledging the perspective of someone who sees things in ways I haven't considered can be very helpful at times.

When you become too rigid about how things are *supposed* to be, you lock yourself out of some very interesting possibilities. A need to control others takes over, and you find yourself becoming hypercritical or unable to trust that anyone else will do the amazing job you can do. However, when you relax and aren't frustrated, judgmental, or overcritical, it's much easier to work with others.

In addition to reducing control-freak tendencies, receiving help requires us to love ourselves even though we don't have what it takes to solve all of our problems by ourselves. Since we're not meant to live in isolation, we're supposed to learn the lessons of give-and-take as we work with others—and that means giving unconditionally, accepting graciously, and requesting assistance when we need it.

As I've mentioned, asking for help can take courage. Men especially tend to resist doing so; they try to solve all their problems on their own because they don't want to be perceived as weak. In fact, far more women than

men seek counseling. My guess is that women have been taught that it's okay to ask for help, but men have been conditioned to believe that they should "suck it up" and find solutions on their own. Yet regardless of our gender, many of us must learn to just respond to an offer of help with a simple "Yes, thank you! I'd really appreciate it if you could do that for me."

All people have insecurities, so you might feel comfortable asking for help in one area, but not in another. If you know that you need assistance but are avoiding asking for it, you're probably afraid. Try to create feelings of courage in yourself, but if you're still slipping back into fearful behavior, ask for help anyway—that very act can reduce your level of anxiety.

Now don't make the mistake of losing faith in yourself simply because you've realized that you have some improvements to make—everyone does! For example, if you don't communicate well with your child, it doesn't make you a bad parent; or if you don't manage your finances well, that doesn't mean you should feel embarrassed because you need someone else to balance your checkbook. The more self-acceptance you feel, the easier it will be for you to admit that you need the aid of others to overcome obstacles on your path to success.

Help Is All Around You

When you're seeking help, you may think, *But I don't know anyone who knows anything about the issue I'm wrestling with.* Well, start talking to people—you might be surprised by their hidden knowledge or their connections to others. For example, I know a freelance editor

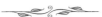
who says that she often gets calls from would-be authors referred to her by friends and family . . . and even her long-time hair stylist. Remember that movie *Six Degrees of Separation?* It was based on the idea that each of us is only six personal connections away from everyone else in the world. *You* might be only one or two degrees away from the very person who can help you.

The Internet has become a marvelous tool for assisting people in finding information and support. Start with a simple search for a term and see where it leads you. There are online forums, support groups, and sites that can help you locate professionals specializing in your specific situation. Facebook and similar social-networking Websites can also connect you to others who share your interests. In fact, more adults are using these sites now than ever before to meet and network with others—not to keep tabs on their teenagers.

Ask for support and you'll soon find reassurance that you aren't alone—lots of people want to help you achieve your goals. You'll see that even complete strangers understand and empathize with what you're going through and are willing to help. (In fact, strangers are sometimes able to be more emotionally and practically supportive than those who are close to you.) As you feel your sense of hope and joy increase, you'll also be inspired to give to others. You'll realize that you're part of a much larger community of people who truly do want to contribute to a better world and bring happiness to others wherever they can. What a wonderful position to be in!

Support usually comes from friends and family, but when those you love are unable to be encouraging about your goals, it can be challenging to remain positive and not feel hurt. One of the lessons I've learned is that when

it comes to negative statements from others, you have to consider the source: some individuals have their own issues that don't allow them to do for their loved ones what they'd like to be able to.

When I was growing up, my parents could be very gruff with me. They were working long hours and raising four kids, and they weren't the type to say to their children, "I'm so proud of you just for being you!" It simply wasn't how they were brought up—my dad, in particular, had a very emotionally difficult childhood. During my youth, people didn't understand how important it was to help children feel cherished, valued, and loved unconditionally. I knew that in their way, my parents loved me and wanted me to know that, but they couldn't give me the support I needed at the time. I finally had to learn to accept that about them.

It can be hard to deal with a lack of approval from others, but when you realize that they aren't going to be there for you, be careful not to create negative feelings about yourself. Depersonalize the situation and do your best to understand them and respect where they're coming from. When you're accepting and loving, you create positive emotions that allow you to discover other possibilities for support. I've known many people who have found incredible encouragement from compassionate men and women they hardly knew.

As you work with others and face challenges, stay true to your Won Thing. When conflicts occur, or you're not sure what to do or which way to turn, look within. Generate positive emotions, and reconnect with your

deepest values and priorities. If you've found that they've changed, then it's time to adjust your Won Thing. Be proud of yourself for your honesty, growth, and willingness to change paths in order to bring your goals closer into alignment with the longings of your heart. Ask for support and reassurance from others whenever you're unsure, but let the final word on what you have to do come from that voice within that's connected to the wisdom of the universe—the one that serves as your inner compass. You have the potential to be a winner in every area of your life, but you must stop looking outside yourself for the winning formula. You, and only you, can define the Won Thing that will create in you a sense of passion, contentment, fulfillment, wonder, success, and eagerness to make your life even better. Do it because you deserve the life you desire!

ACKNOWLEDGMENTS

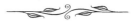

Writing a book is one thing (excuse the reference to "one thing"—smile), but writing the Acknowledgments is a challenge—at least it is for me. There are so many people who deserve recognition, and I know that a page or two doesn't suffice for expressing thanks to all who have given me the immeasurable support I'm grateful to receive.

My life is blessed with two special men: my son, Michel, and my husband, Denis. Both of these men gently remind me to stay true to the messages in this book and to live with purpose and clarity so that I might feel fulfilled. With them in my life, there's no other way for me to be.

To Nancy Peske, the talented co-creator of this book (and many others) . . . thank *you!* If you hear me speak about Nancy, you'll hear gushing praise and glowing comments about her. Nancy is a gift from God—an angel on Earth—helping me deliver important messages to my readers worldwide.

My devoted, giving, bighearted agent, Cathy Hemming, is another shining light in this world and in my life. She believes in me, offers endless support, never judges, always gives, and is unconditionally loving. I adore how she concludes her e-mails with "your faithful agent, love you, Cathy."

My gratitude abounds for the incredibly talented group of editors Hay House has provided me: Jill Kramer,

Alex Freemon, Shannon Littrell, and Patrick Gabrysiak. Thank you for putting your heart and soul into your work and creating a ripple of good in this world.

To the marketing machine behind the Internet-launch campaigns for my books, led by my sister Judy O'Beirn, my sweet niece Jennifer Gibson, my other adorable niece Amy Lusk, and the lovely Yvonne Higham. Thank you for the tremendous support and the endless amount of work you put into creating successful launches to help get these books into the hands of those who enjoy them the most.

Every week I meet with my dear and special friend Arielle Ford, who also happens to be my mastermind buddy. She supports me, encourages me, guides me, and has a brilliant marketing mind! Most important, though, is her loving spirit. Arielle unconditionally gives more than anyone I've ever met.

My million-book mastermind group has been, and continues to be, wonderful support and a cherished group of great friends. Arielle is part of this, too! I'm grateful to be associated with an incredible bunch of talented visionaries, leaders, authors, and speakers who include: John Assaraf, Marci Shimoff, Ken Foster, Debbie Ford, Gay Hendricks, and Greg Reid. Thank you for the continual support and the brilliant insights you provide.

Thank you, my "Won Thing" teachers: Bob Proctor, Zig Ziglar, Deepak Chopra, Louise Hay, Wayne Dyer, Neale Donald Walsch, Og Mandino, Tony Robbins, and many others!

And, I'm grateful to you, dear reader, and to the clients I am blessed to serve.

ABOUT THE AUTHOR

A *New York Times* best-selling author and an internationally recognized expert in the area of goal achievement, **Peggy McColl** has been inspiring individuals, professional athletes, and organizations to realize their goals and reach their maximum potential for the past 25 years. She is the president and founder of Dynamic Destinies, Inc., an organization that trains authors, entrepreneurs, corporate leaders, and employees in some of the most compelling and strategic goal-setting technologies of our times.

Peggy is the author of the *New York Times* bestsellers *Your Destiny Switch, 21 Distinctions of Wealth, Be a Dog with a Bone, On Being . . . The Creator of Your Destiny,* and *The 8 Proven Secrets to SMART Success.*

For more information about Peggy and her work, visit: **www.destinies.com**.

NOTES

NOTES

NOTES

NOTES

We hope you enjoyed this Hay House book.
If you'd like to receive our online catalog featuring
additional information on Hay House books
and products, or if you'd like to find out more
about the Hay Foundation, please contact:

Hay House, Inc.
P.O. Box 5100
Carlsbad, CA 92018-5100

(760) 431-7695 or (800) 654-5126
(760) 431-6948 (fax) or (800) 650-5115 (fax)
www.hayhouse.com® • www.hayfoundation.org

Published and distributed in Australia by: Hay House Australia Pty.
Ltd., 18/36 Ralph St., Alexandria NSW 2015 • *Phone:* 612-9669-4299
Fax: 612-9669-4144 • www.hayhouse.com.au

Published and distributed in the United Kingdom by:
Hay House UK, Ltd., 292B Kensal Rd., London W10 5BE • *Phone:*
44-20-8962-1230 • *Fax:* 44-20-8962-1239 • www.hayhouse.co.uk

Published and distributed in the Republic of South Africa by:
Hay House SA (Pty), Ltd., P.O. Box 990, Witkoppen 2068 • *Phone/Fax:*
27-11-467-8904 • info@hayhouse.co.za • www.hayhouse.co.za

Published in India by: Hay House Publishers India, Muskaan
Complex, Plot No. 3, B-2, Vasant Kunj, New Delhi 110 070 • *Phone:*
91-11-4176-1620 • *Fax:* 91-11-4176-1630 • www.hayhouse.co.in

Distributed in Canada by: Raincoast, 9050 Shaughnessy St.,
Vancouver, B.C. V6P 6E5 • *Phone:* (604) 323-7100
Fax: (604) 323-2600 • www.raincoast.com

Take Your Soul on a Vacation

Visit **www.HealYourLife.com**® to regroup,
recharge, and reconnect with your own magnificence.
Featuring blogs, mind-body-spirit news, and
life-changing wisdom from Louise Hay and friends.

Visit **www.HealYourLife.com** today!